New Revised Edition

How to
Self Publish
and make money

D0048210

Marion Crook & Nancy Wise
Sandhill Publishing/Crook Publishing
1997

Canadian Cataloguing in Publication Data
Crook, Marion, 1941-
      How to self publish and make money:
writing, publishing and selling in Canada
Rev. ed.
Includes index
ISBN 0-920923-10-0
      1. Self-publishing. I. Wise, Nancy II. Title
Z285.5.C76 1996 070.5'93   C96-900834-1

Distributed by:
Sandhill Book Marketing Ltd.
#99-1270 Ellis Street,
Kelowna, British Columbia V1Y 1Z4
Ph: 250-763-1406 Fax: 250-763-4051

Cover artwork by Jack Thompson. Edited by Brian Scrivener
Production by Nancy Wise
First printing 1997 Second Printing 1999

Printed and bound in Canada by Hignell Printing Ltd.

Preface to Second Edition

In the years since this book has been in print the authors have enjoyed the vitality and enthusiasm that increasing numbers of self published authors are bringing to the industry. More and more authors are carefully researching the book industry and finding a place for themselves and their books.

We have seen a change in the way these books are being received. With the growing improvement in the quality of self published books, booksellers are recognizing the value of this form of publishing. The taint of vanity and "ego" publishing has lessened and self publishing finally is considered a legitimate and profitable venture. While the thrill of being a pioneer, braving the tides of controversy, rebelling against the status quo and conquering prejudice has lessened, the excitement of creation is still strong. We know that this book will help you understand the publishing world, your place in it, your chances of success and help you plan how to produce the book that exists in such splendour in your mind.

Think of this book as a travel guide on your journey into the complex world of writing, publishing and selling books. Like a travel guide, some parts will have more impact than others and some will be more important in different stages of your production. We hope it will serve you well and make your voyage into the Canadian book industry a smooth one.

It is impossible to mention here the many people who have contributed to our experiences in the book industry. The encouragement of many is much appreciated in spurring us on in the completion of this new, revised edition. In particular, we wish to thank the following for their enthusiasm, help, and/or point of view:

Don Barnicki, Jan Bauman, A.J. Beddie, Herb Brent Sharon Clark, Bill Crook, Glen Crook, Wilma Dohler James Irvine, Jim Korchinski, Heidi LeRossignol, Margaret Lye, Rhoda Moss, Michael Neill, Michele Neill, Linda Palmer, Margaret Reynolds, Brian Scrivener, Murphy Shewchuk, Jack Thompson, Chelsea Wise.

Contents

Press Releases • Where to Send Your Press Releases • Some Tips
on Media Interviews • Space Ads • Benefits of Media Publicity
Sustaining Your Market • The Internet as a Form of Publicity

Dial 911 • The Days of Wine and Roses • Standard Trade Terms
Changes in Buying Trends • Problems Facing Self Publishers
Handling Sales: Small Press Runs • Consignment Sales • Guaran-
teed Sales • How to Write an Invoice • Goods and Services Tax
Shipping Charges • Packing Orders • Making Sales Projections
Handling Sales: Large Press Runs • The Sales Representative
Distributors • Parallel Lines of Distribution • Wholesalers • Take
My Book, Please • Patience and Perseverance

PART ONE:

Why Publish?

Marion Crook

Getting Started $\qquad$ 1

THE COMPULSION TO WRITE

Authors write for obvious reasons such as recording historic information or preserving a family saga, but we also write for less obvious reasons. We may feel a need to control some part of the world by creating a fictional one. We yearn for immortality in print. Or we have a special skill or special knowledge that we want to share with others and need to write a "how to" book on that subject. Whatever our reasons, they are enough to drive our writing. Many of us must write. We have an irritating, unreasonable, socially isolating and compelling need to create stories.

Satisfaction

Some writers are satisfied if they get the words on the page and don't care if their creation is filed in a cardboard box and left unread in the basement. That isn't enough for most writers. Most of us write to imaginary readers who are important to us. We need to communicate, intimately, honestly and often.

Writers differ in what will satisfy this need. You might be satisfied to compile your family history and watch your sons and daughters and grandsons and granddaughters read it. You might be happy only if the whole community is reading it. You might feel frustrated and unfulfilled until everyone in North America is reading it. You share the compulsion to write with many, but your level of satisfaction is unique.

Self-examination

You need to understand why you write before you can decide if you need to publish. Ask yourself the following questions:

- Do I know what I want to say?
- Do I have a unique point of view?
- Do I think about this subject in a way that differs from most people?
- Do I have special knowledge of this subject?
- Do others want to know about it?
- If I brought up the subject to others would they ask me many questions about it?
- Will I still be interested in this subject in a year?

It is common to believe that just because you can speak a language, you can write it. Assess your own skills and take a writing course to learn more. Some continuing education institutions offer writing and publishing courses. Some are one-time courses available to anyone interested and some are defined programs leading to degrees. Ask yourself:

- Do I have writing skills?
- Can I see the book as a whole with sub-texts, underlying questions, possible side-issues and interesting developments?

It also is important to consider alternatives to books. Is there a better way to communicate this material through film, radio, brochures, letters-to-the-editor?

If you decide that you must write, that you have a sustaining interest, unique perspective and creative energy that will only be satisfied by writing, then you have to ask yourself the ultimate question—do you want to publish?

REASONS FOR PUBLISHING

Large publishing houses have strong commercial reasons for publishing: the book must appeal to many people, it must reflect the current social values, it must be promotable. As a self publisher you may have strong commercial reasons for publishing but you also may have different reasons. You may want to produce lively, interesting books that appeal to few but are a unique contribution to the book industry. You may want to give the reading public a choice among a variety of books, among a bubbling, creative field of new ideas. You may want the brief history of Clyde MacDonald, plumber extraordinaire, the French Creek Community's report on wild birds of the Atlantic coast, the philosophy of the Pemberton Valley Metaphysical Association. Most commercial publishers began their career with just such reasons as this. They felt they had to publish this one book. One book led to many.

You have read many books—and it is important that you read many books on your subject—and you realize that the large commercial publishers do not necessarily publish books of great literary merit, nor do they publish books that necessarily reflect the needs of the public. Publishers large and small are generally bound by the financial limits governing the sale of a tremendous volume of books. If they think a book will make good profits, it has a chance of being published; and, generally, if they think a book won't make money, it won't be published. A self publisher also must consider similar economic limits, but you can respond to a smaller public need. You don't have to address your books to a mass audience because you may target a small group of readers. Your profit margin may not need to be as great as a commercial publisher's, and you may be able to slide it according to the variables you meet as you make your publishing judgements. We assume, in this book, that you don't want to lose money.

Speed

You want to self publish because you have a book that must reach the market this year. Few publishers will put it out earlier than one or two years hence. Publishers usually have a marketing plan that includes a commitment to produce certain books over the next two, five or ten years. Occasionally, a publisher will see a book he or she wants to publish, and design a marketing program to include it quickly. But, usually, a book will have to wait until editors are free to give it attention. That may be in a year or two.

Control

You want to self publish because you want to control the design and content of the book. You, the publisher, will control the design, cover, content, promotion and marketing.

This is the reason for publishing that appealed to me. In some ways, this is a license to make mistakes, but it is certainly interesting. You, as the publisher, hire a cover designer, an editor and choose your own title. You arrange for the printing, the distribution and the promotion. You then feel that the sales of the book are a result of your decisions. The lack of sales are also your problem, but the project is all yours. You share the satisfaction of creating a book with all publishers, whether they are author-publishers or unrelated owners of big companies. All are proud of their productions. It is akin to giving birth to a baby, for it has the same sense of surprised accomplishment.

Gain

You want to self publish because you want to make money. All publishers want to make money—enough money to produce another book. A publisher once told me that publishing was a very "seductive"' business. She was right. You finish one book and plan for the next, always thinking that the next book will be the great book—and a money-maker. Publishing shares some aspects of a lottery game. You're sure next week is going to be the big week. There may be a few publishers who want only to break even, not lose money, and I did meet one man who felt that publishing a book was such an interesting experience he didn't mind paying for it, but most of us need to make money. This book is written with the assumption that you, the reader, can't afford to lose.

Certainty

You want to self publish because you have tried to sell your manuscript and no publisher will buy it. Sometimes publishers won't take a manuscript because it is badly written. But it is wrong

6

to assume that that is the only reason that manuscripts are not accepted. Publishers' programs often do not allow room for any book that does not precisely fit their program criteria. Even if your manuscript is on gardening and the publisher regularly publishes gardening books, his publishing program for the next five years might be so specific—small plot gardening—for instance that your proposed book, *Getting the Most From Your Acreage*, won't fit. Publishers establish promotion budgets and try to cover as many books with one budget as possible. They find it more cost effective to promote a series of boating books than to promote one boating book, one sewing book and one child care book. Your manuscript may cost a publisher too much to promote when his promotion focus is elsewhere.

Why Not To Publish

Consider why your book may not be published. Your writing may be good but your subject not appropriate. Publishers reject manuscripts because the book is too costly to produce. It may have many colour photographs and could cost more than the publisher foresees returned.

Some books are libelous and too risky to publish. Some books are the opinion of an author who has no academic or professional qualifications to weight his opinion.

If your book is rejected for some of the above reasons, perhaps you should think twice about publishing it yourself. Judge whether the commercial publisher's reasons for not publishing are also good reasons for you not to publish.

Ego

You want to self publish because you want to see your name on a bookshelf. This is not the best reason for publishing. On the other hand, some ego involvement in your book is essential. You should believe in your work the way an artist believes in his painting, the way a mechanic believes in the engine he worked on, the way all artisans feel toward their work. You must have some strong feelings about your manuscript. All publishing involves ego in the same sense all creative work does. If your only reason for publishing is to be known as an author and to see your name in print, then you need either a very small run or a vanity press, a company you pay to publish. You must consider whether your need is great enough to consume the time, money and effort that self publishing is going require.

Satisfaction

Self published books, on the other hand, are a commercial enterprise. You, the self publisher, take the same risks as any publisher. You make the same decisions, are faced with the same problems of moving inventory. You are vitally interested in the quality of the writing and hire an editor to comment on it. The book is yours; it reflects your judgement; it is one hundred percent your effort. It is not necessary for you to actually "do it all yourself." You can, but most publishers don't. If you plan the book and hire help, the book is yours in much the same way that the building designed by the architect and built by sub-contractors, remains the possession of the owner.

Your Time

When you are considering self publishing, remember that publishing takes time, and it takes time away from writing. Will your publishing activities stimulate your personality and make you a better writer? Will your writing activities make you a better publisher? Or will each activity draw from the other until you are neither a good publisher nor a good writer? Do you have the time to sell your book? Will you go store to store with it? Do you have time to promote, collect orders and send out books? Or, perhaps, will the whole experience help prepare you for a career in the book industry? Do your soul-searching before you publish. Decide how you want to spend your time.

MARKETS
Instant Markets

Because you appear weekly on a television show, you want to publish a book to sell directly to your television audience. You already have fame, you want to capitalize on your notoriety with a book. You need to assess the size of your market, but you can be reasonably assured that there is interest in your subject.

You may be presenting a series of lectures or you may regularly teach a certain subject. You have many notes and you have presented the material so many times you know what particular sections of your material interests your audience. You not only have much of your research done, you have an audience which may buy directly from you. You also may have established a reputation as an expert which will give credibility to the book. You then have reasonably good assurance of sales—some sales.

What Is Your Market?

You must give much thought to the size and nature of your market. If you decide to self publish your book on *Original Weaving Patterns of the Kettle Valley* because your local weavers group needs to have all the patterns in one book, you must then decide how many people are interested in that subject and tailor your production to that number. If you decide to publish a history of your family and your family numbers six hundred and five, then print six hundred. If your family is first cousin to the Queen of England you might have a bigger market. If you think you have unique information about why diets are unhealthy then decide how many people you want to reach with a book on this topic. Do you want to change the eating habits of your town, your province or the whole country? Your motivation shapes your product and your sales. If you decide you have a huge market—parents of teenagers, all parents of all teenagers in North America—you must find some reason why those parents would buy your book rather than one by Bill Cosby. What is it about your book that gives you the edge in the market? And how will you reach that market?

There is really no substitute for the knowledge you gain by talking to the people who will read and use your book. When you listen to those who will form your buying public, you learn what they need, what interests them and what opportunities there are in this market. I also find this process of listening most educational for I discover more about the subject I'm investigating, my audience becomes my teacher and my resulting manuscript is richer, broader, more interesting and more saleable.

RESEARCHING YOUR MARKET
Defining Your Subject

You must understand exactly what you are writing about and how you are treating your subject. If you decide to write a book about shoplifting, are you going to write about it from the point of view of the shop-lifter, or the law, or society? Be sure you understand who you want to read your book and from which point of view. Establishing this early avoids costly editing and revising and saves hours and days, even months of writing time. After you have defined your end user, write for that market.

WRITING FOR YOUR MARKET
The Educational Market

The educational market encompasses primary and secondary schools, colleges and universities. If you write for this market, you need to understand what the buyers want. If you are a teacher, you may have a "curriculum guide" that tells you what each grade is studying. Non-teachers can write to the Department of Education in their provinces for these guides. With such a guide you can know, for instance, that buyers will be more likely to buy a children's novel set in a prairie historical settlement if the age group you are writing for is studying prairie settlements. You also need to understand "readability levels", or the complexity of language appropriate for defined ages. As well, you need to know the kinds of material buyers are looking for. Bookbuyers for elementary and high schools are looking for fiction with protagonists that are usually two years older than the readers who live the adventure. The protagonist should have a sense of control over their lives. The buyers prefer books set in Canada with situations that reflect the uniqueness of an area. Different age levels look for different kinds of writing, setting and characters. Non-fiction for the educational market needs to be written in a way that allows the reader to remain interested throughout. Writing classes will help you develop specific skills that convey your ideas in ways that appeal to your readers, but you need to read the material bought by the educational market to assess and analyze what it contains.

Libraries

Librarians are usually interested in new books, have little prejudice against self published books and respond to your sales approach on the basis of their public's need. They know their reading public well and know if a new gardening book, a new fishing book or a new baby-care book will be used in their library. Librarians are good critics of writing styles and skills and can give you advice on what books they believe are well-written and what books the public likes.

Special Interest Groups

A book on the history of wild mushrooms of the Thompson Valley would be a special interest book if you published the book specifically for the Mushroom Club of the Thompson Valley and expected to sell the whole press run to the club as a single bulk sale. You may have a wider appeal and may be able to sell into other mushroom clubs or horticultural societies across the country, or the book may be so well illustrated that it becomes a collector's work of art. Anything is possible.

When writing for a special interest group you have a chance to work with an advisory committee. I suggest you submit an outline of your book to such a committee and ask for comments before you begin to write. That way, you can include their advice. The Mushroom Growers group may advise you that they want to see a section on new strains of mushrooms. By listening to them and incorporating that information as they request, you broaden your book and increase your sales. You may find that by responding positively to their advice you make your book more attractive to more readers. Perhaps you will be invited to speak to an international conference because this information is important to many.

Corporate interests can motivate special interest groups. As with other special interest groups, you must listen to the company and find out what they want from your book. Research is very important here. You will need to submit a detailed outline to the company for their approval. This is an excellent opportunity to ask for names of company representatives whom you can interview. From such a list of contacts, you can get further recommendations and extend your research. Ask the company for archival material

11

and try to work with an employee who understands it. Once you have the company's view of itself, try to expand your research contacts to see how the company interacts with its environment and how it fits into the community. Once you have your information, decide on your point of view and start writing. Check with your company contacts, or better yet an advisory committee from the company, after two chapters to ensure that you have their support. When the book is ready the company should be ready to accept the advance orders they placed. This is, of course, only one way to work with a corporate client.

The Trade Market

The trade book market encompasses everything from perfect bound 6 by 9 inch soft cover books, to large, hard-cover coffee table picture books. These are the books you find in bookstores, gift shops and some grocery stores. The trade book market is a highly competitive sales field that requires study. It is important that you research this market. (See page 89 for more on markets.)

You will find yourself familiar with the shelves of the local bookstore that carries the kind of book you want to write. You might have memorized their selection by now. Study the books. When I was asked to write a book for eight to twelve year olds and I hadn't written for that age group in five years, I bought books that the bookseller assured me were selling well and read them. I asked my local librarian to recommend books that were most popular in that age group and took all fifteen home to read. I analyzed them and tried to see why the readers liked them before I started to write. When the manuscript was ready, I asked a young reader to criticize it. Remember that your readers may not want to hurt your feelings, so learn to distinguish between "It's nice," and "It's fantastic!"

The non-fiction trade market requires factual research. You are the credible authority of your book, so phone national organizations and get on the mailing list of groups in your area that are interested in your subject. Go to conferences. Listen. Absorb. Learn. Then put your unique point of view on the information and write. Nancy will give you the information on how your ideas need to fit into the retail market later in this book. I tell you that, as the writer of the book, you need to have a publisher's awareness of what will sell and what will not, what the market will welcome and what it will reject.

If you can, try to sell articles in magazines, newspapers or radio that can establish your credibility in your field. This makes promoting and selling your book much easier. And, if you sell to another publisher, it will make your manuscript more attractive.

ATTITUDES
The Negatives

You may hear a chorus of advice when you decide to self publish. "You'll lose money." "You won't be able to market the book." "You don't know how to publish a book." Well, all that may be true. But this book will help you avoid all three problems. My first self published book was close to an economic disaster, but it allowed me to learn what I needed to know to be successful with the next five. Learn from my mistakes; don't make your own. With a good publishing plan you won't need a disaster to be successful.

The Positives

You need confidence to solve the many problems that pop up like construction zones on a freeway. You must be able to deal with each slow-down as a temporary problem and not a road block. Whatever your ability to be tenacious, it should be increased and well-developed by the time your book hits the shelves. Above all, be enthusiastic about your book. Authors are, very often, the greatest sellers of their wares. Most readers and booksellers are eager to talk to an author. Tell them what a marvellous book it is. If you don't, who will? If you didn't think it was good you would not have published it. Try to keep your anxieties about the book to yourself. Be enthusiastic. Enthusiasm stimulates contacts with other publishers, with distributors and with media personnel. It stimulates promotional ideas. It stimulates other people's involvement in your book. If you are enthusiastic about your book, others are inspired to read it—and buy it. Never say negative things about your own book. Everyone understands that no published book is perfect. Even if you think it's perfect, someone will debate parts of it. It isn't necessary for you to point out the book's faults. What may seem to you to be modest, self-effacement looks to others like lack

13

of self confidence. It is wise to be realistic about your book's faults, privately, so you can avoid them in the next book, but do not point out its problems to others. There is something positive to say about your book or you would not have published it.

Attitudes of the Industry to Self Publishing

The booksellers and bookbuyers of this country are often wary of self published books. A self published book does not have the seal of approval of a publishing house. Bookbuyers rely on publishing house editors to screen out non-saleable items. Self published books have avoided this screening process. In spite of this, most bookbuyers will look twice at a self published book in the hope that it is the unique, surprising, outstanding exception. And sometimes it is—as proved by David Chilton's *The Wealthy Barber* which continues as an international bestseller.

Booksellers may look on self publishing as a kind of vanity press or ego publishing—brash and aggressive with overtones of conceit. Artists who paint, matt, frame and sell their pictures seldom endure this criticism. You may begin to feel that there is something reprehensible about publishing your own work. Take heart. Mark Twain, after his successful experience with *Tom Sawyer* with a commercial publishing house, self published *Huckleberry Finn*. Walt Whitman was an intrepid hustler of his own work, *Leaves of Grass*, even going so far as to write his own reviews. Every January there is a special festival to honour the poet Robbie Burns whose motive for self publishing *Poems Chiefly in the Scottish Dialect* was to earn the nine guineas he needed for passage to a new life in Jamaica. That effort was so profitable that he changed his embarkation plans. Beatrix Potter self published *The Tale of Peter Rabbit*, one of the world's most popular children's stories. Jean Pare, *Company's Coming* cookbooks first published out of Vermillion, Alberta, produced an initial run of her third book, *Salads*, of seventy-five thousand copies. Her book *150 Delicious Squares* has sold seven hundred and fifty thousand copies. Together, all her titles have sold 10 million copies. This is remarkable for a self published author. There are some success stories. As a self published author you will be in excellent company.

14

SETTING GOALS

Once you have decided why you are writing and publishing take the time to work out, step-by-step, exactly what you are going to do. Setting goals becomes a time-consuming, irritating exercise that dogs the whole process of writing and publishing. You should constantly define your goals and reassess them, check to make sure you are making decisions based on your goals and generally use them as the structure for your activities.

What do you want to achieve by a set date? Do you want to publish and sell one thousand books locally by next October? Do you want to publish and distribute five thousand books by next August? Do you want to hand print three hundred copies of a book of Haiku to sell from one gift shop in your home town? You can look at one idea, the *Wild Mushrooms of the Thompson Valley*, for instance, and set different goals for it. You can decide to publish five hundred copies of a mushroom guide for your mushroom club, or you can decide to publish five thousand perfect bound trade books with full colour pictures for the International Mushroom Fanciers Conference, or two thousand copies for the trade book market plus several thousand to the I.M.F.C. You need to set your goals very early so that you will waste neither time, money nor effort on your publishing project. By now you know what you want and why you want to write and publish. With that information you can decide how many books you should produce, and what quality of production you need.

Start small. I didn't. I started huge with five thousand copies of a book of fiction and no market. Don't do that. It ages you. Start with a market you know you can handle. If five hundred copies of your mushroom book will be easy to sell, make five hundred copies practical by reducing the costs of production and doing your own distribution. Don't try to crack the world market on your first effort. You can re-print your book, upgrading it if the market demands. Many self publishers make the mistake of putting out thousands of a good quality book with high unit cost and no method of getting the money back except a vague hope that the books will sell. It isn't wise to operate that way. Keep your goals manageable.

In the last ten years some excellent programs have been

offered that give you advice and encouragement in publishing. Some universities offer courses and some continuing educational institutions offer one day or evening classes. Both Nancy and I have taught such courses and find the students exciting and talented. Look in the papers or inquire at the library for lists of courses in your area. Such courses also offer the support of colleagues.

REWARDS

Most people require positive reinforcement to achieve a goal. You know yourself best, but don't underestimate the need for rewards. Publishing can be a lonely, discouraging business. No one but you knows how hard you're working, how much you have to do, how discouraging it can be to try. Look ahead and plan to give yourself encouragement at first, frequent encouragement because the reward of completing the book may seem too far away. It is essential to be tenacious, and rewarding yourself is one way of helping you stay with the project. Eventually, the final payment on your loan should you have one may be your reward and, for quite a while, even meeting the interest payments may feel like an accomplishment. At the end of the project, a glimpse of the finished book may make it all worth while. But, in the meantime, remember that you are the boss and the worker and you need enough energy to stay with the publishing project to it's finish.

WHAT'S OUT THERE
The Need For Your Book

You know what you want to publish and why. Now find out what's been written in your field. If possible use your computer or your friend's computer and call up local libraries searching by title and subject. Or walk into the library and use their computer. Visit several bookstores looking for books on your subject. You are looking for holes in the market, blank spots in your subject area that no one has touched. When you research information on your subject you may miss any book that is in progress and you may find on your publishing date that another publishing house is releasing a similar book. That may happen and occasionally does happen, but it is rare unless books are published around a certain popular event such as a national or international sports tournament.

16

Competition

It is wonderful to research a market and find that no one has ever written a book on your subject. Well, it can be wonderful. You have to decide whether no one has written a book because they haven't thought of it, or because it won't sell. Talk to booksellers. Ask them what books on your subject do sell. Look at the books they offer on your subject and ask the bookseller which ones are most popular. Study these. If you find that the *National Geographic* has a beautiful hard cover, full colour book on weavers of the Kettle Valley, you'd better not offer yours. Save yourself time and money and choose another subject to write about. The exception to this rule seems to be cookbooks. There must be thousands of cookbooks and hundreds more arriving every year, but, generally, if a good book is readily available in bookstores on your subject, leave the subject alone. Try something else.

You will discover the wonderful world of government funding that seems to be available for all publishers except you. Self publishers do not qualify for subsidy. Your price reflects your costs; the larger houses' price reflects their costs minus their subsidy. If you publish a book on a subject that has already been covered by the large publishing house, your costs will be higher and your price may be higher. Or, even if your price is similar, their distribution will be wider and their publicity may be more efficient and wide-spread. You may not be able to compete. Pick a subject they haven't touched. If there is room in the market for a book in a different format than is already published or at a different price and you still want to publish your book, try your idea on knowledgeable people in the book trade and listen to their advice. You may go ahead against their advice, but get it anyway. Who would ever have thought that *101 Uses of a Dead Cat* would ever sell? One of the joys of publishing is the strange success of eccentric ideas.

The Present Market

You can get ideas about new book designs, covers and new trends in your subject area by studying the shelves of bookstores. Read the catalogues put out seasonally by publishing houses. They may be available in your local library. Subscribe to publications or magazines with information about the book industry. In Canada, the *Quill and Quire* is a trade publication of "book news and reviews"available for purchase on newsstands and in bookstores. *BC Bookworld* and *Prairie Books Now* are two other regional publications that offer information about new books. Read such resources thoroughly. You will find the new books being proposed for each season as well as information about trade shows, and discussions on problems in the industry. Most libraries subscribe to the many trade magazines and tabloids.

Advice of Special Interest Groups

If you do involve groups in your research, as suggested earlier, you will find them interested in purchasing your book. It makes good sense to consult such groups for information and for future markets. If your motive for publishing is to provide a book for your small group of six hundred enthusiasts, then research the needs of those six hundred as thoroughly as you can so that your book is exactly the book they need. If you decide to write your philosophy on love and marriage and feel that there are probably five hundred people who would read it, you still must reach those five hundred and must spend some time deciding how you are going to do that: a notice in your church bulletin? an ad in the local paper? pamphlets at the family counselling center? Keep a list of potential markets and note the date you contacted them and what results you achieved. Write letters informing those in your market of the book's imminent production and assess your print run from the answers you receive. If no one answers your inquiries keep your print run at your original estimate to service your original market. If you are flooded with inquiries, increase your print run or plan to print again soon.

Other Books On Your Subject

You have studied other books on your subject and analyzed them. What did they not include that you think is necessary? What was wrong with their approach? How do you think you can improve on what they are doing? If you can't, your book will be hard to sell. If you can, then you tell the bookbuyer why your book is better. You will know. You will have studied the opposition. I keep small cards of titles and authors with a synopsis of their book and comments that will allow me to avoid their problems. I might write "Don't italicize in every paragraph. It drives the reader crazy." Or I'll comment on the subject matter: lack of depth, lack of detail, confusing organization. This study gives me information about my subject, tells me exactly what the reader's choices are in the field and points out improvements that I can make for my book. It also gives me confidence in the marketplace after the book is produced. Sometimes it is difficult to remember who wrote what. After I had written the book *Teenagers Talk About Adoption* and after I had read all kinds of books on the whole field of adoption, I certainly couldn't remember all of the books and who had written them, but I had a good idea of what had been offered to the readers. This study gave me confidence that no one had yet offered my point of view or my information. That confidence was a great help when I was on a promotional tour of radio, television and speaking engagements.

Potential Customers

If you travel very much be aware of spots where you could place your book. If you travel to mushroom conferences make arrangements with the conference organizers or a bookstore in the conference city to have your book for sale at next year's conference. Or ask them to include you as a speaker at next year's conference. Find out if there is a possibility of selling books in a series of conferences. Be alert to opportunities. Get their mailing list! Find out before you publish the book if bookstores or special interest groups are truly interested in your subject. Yes, of course there are exceptions. If Percy Bysshe Shelley had not self published, his poems might still be undiscovered. Zane Grey may have died a dentist if he had not self published *Betty Zane* in 1904. His *Riders of the Purple Sage* has sold five million copies. In those cases the authors may have had more faith than facts to motivate them, but, in most cases, good research of the market is important to sales.

Advice from the Book Industry

All booksellers, librarians, sales representatives, publishers, authors, and printers have opinions on books. Listen to them. Much of what is known about what makes a book interesting and desirable is not available in print. Those who work in the field of publishing can tell you which distributor is effective, what format they think works for your book and why, what titles sell best for them, what colours seem most attractive, what markets are opening. Take the time to listen to others in the business. They have very valuable information, but remember that their time is valuable, too—it's often wise to make an appointment in advance for a lengthy discussion. Often the person you are talking to today is the person who changes jobs and becomes someone who can assist you greatly in the future. The Canadian publishing community is relatively small. In time, you may know many of the principals of other companies and be privy to much help.

PART TWO:
The Manuscript

Marion Crook

Creating
the Manuscript   2

PREPARATION

You have decided what to write, you know why you are writing and you have researched the market's need for your book. Now you are ready to write it. Not quite. You need to research your subject.

All subjects, fiction or non-fiction, must be accurately researched. Some writers spend months researching their subject before they start writing. They crawl through the stacks in the libraries, search newspaper clippings on aspects of their subject, do interviews with experts and study books. This is a valid and useful way to begin, but not every writer's way. When I write fiction, I usually write descriptions of the main characters and the setting as well as the first chapter before I start the research. When I write non-fiction, I do enough reading to understand the field I will be investigating, then write an outline before beginning the research. *A Question of Justice 1886* required months in the Vancouver, B.C. archives. There was little easy information and I had to dig into files and compare stories to get facts. The setting was Vancouver June 1886 and the book required accurate research on the physical landmarks of the city, the politics of the day, the state of the C.P.R. railroad construction, the attitude of society to woman, to men, to children, to minorities and what minorities. (Black people were accepted; Chinese were not.) In *The Gulf Island Connection* the story required research on the cocaine trade in British Columbia. Staff Sergeant Scotty Gardiner, that month retired from the Royal Canadian Mounted Police as head of the B.C. Drug Squad, gave me a long, informative, fascinating interview on policing the cocaine market. A body floats into the story and I needed to know exactly how a body would look after three days in the ocean, and how the police would handle it. Sergeant Karel Chizeck, R.C.M.P. Identification Branch, Victoria, gave me the facts in an interview. *Teenagers Talk About Adoption* required five months of steady interviewing with teenagers, social workers, adoptive parents and women who had given children up for adoption. *Teenagers Talk About Suicide* took about a year of interviewing. Like many authors, I find research part of the fascination of writing and have to discipline myself to call a halt to finding out and actually get down to the writing.

COMMITMENT

Once you start writing, you must feel a great sense of commitment to your book. You must feel urgency, a sense that it is important that you finish this book so that it becomes the best book available on the subject. You'll need that drive and discipline. Then you must set more goals, writing goals. You plan to have the first five chapters complete by a certain date. The next five by a certain date. Get out your calendar and make practical plans for writing. If you plan to write every morning and know that your daughter (as happened to a mystery writer friend of mine) has to leave the baby with you four mornings a week, you are not going to get your writing done. Either don't babysit, or plan your writing for later. If you plan three chapters this month and your mother is coming to stay, or it happens to be hunting season and you are scheduled for four goose hunts, or you are moving house to another city, you know you won't do three chapters. If you work full time at another job, will you ever have time to write? Be reasonable. Take a monthly calendar and write in exactly when you are going to write and how much you are going to accomplish.

When you sit down to write, it is surprising how many

distractions, perfectly legitimate distractions, jump in front of you and keep you away from your typing. The room's too cold, the room's too warm, the telephone rings (even with voice mail, I can't resist picking up a ringing phone). A written schedule helps to make each writing period important. When you realize that not working today affects the results at the end of the month, you are more likely to insist that you work when you are scheduled to work. Your family is also more understanding of your need to work today!

PRESENTATION

The physical appearance of the manuscript is important. Decide on a format when you start and stay with it. Decide where your headings will go, the placement of the sub-titles, what margins you'll use, whether you'll start flush with the page or indent—the many decisions that go into the design of the page. Again, check the books already published to find a format that you admire. You may like the way one book is organized; you may like the type face, the font, in another. And, while a neat presentation will not transform a badly written book into a masterpiece, a neat presentation will certainly help you read through it. You want a format that makes reading easy and mistakes obvious, so you can eliminate them early in the process. Publishers and printers will take your format and change it, so you do not need to match theirs, but you do need to decide what works well for you. Publishers and printers will ask you for your disk and your hard copy, that is your paper manuscript, and prefer it to be on good quality, not flimsy, paper. Check before you start typing to be sure that your software is compatible with the printer's machine. There are computer programs that can convert your incompatible disk to one that can be used, but make sure that is possible in your case before you spend months working on a little-known or used software program that can't be converted.

Manuscripts that are typewritten are usually printed on 8.5 by 11 inch good quality bond. Type or print out approximately two hundred and fifty words to a page, double spaced. Don't staple the manuscript, but put all pages, numbered consecutively, loosely into a box. The editor, publisher and printer will appreciate a clear, clean manuscript. Don't think of yourself as writing in an isolated nest away from the rest of the book industry. Think of yourself as the beginning of a long chain of people who will be part of the publishing process. Your first manuscript will be seen by many. Make it attractive and use computer software that will be compatible, or at least convertible to what is standard for the industry. (See page 56 for more on computers and compatibility)

Some authors do not use word processors at all, but they are becoming rare. My first three books were written on an Olivetti manual typewriter, my next two on an I.B.M. Selectric. The rest on a word processor which, I estimated, saved me about forty days of typing per year.

Try to save all versions of your manuscript. One of the problems in using word processors is the practise of deleting an original paragraph when doing a re-write. You may decide four versions of the paragraph later that the original paragraph was the best. So try to print out frequently. It is possible to use a word processor without ever understanding computers in much the same way that it is possible to drive a car without ever understanding the engine. Word processors can be operated successfully with the same kind of ignorance. You only need to know what keys to push, not how the bits and bytes work. It does help to understand how your program works—what it can do, how it can save you time—so you are more efficient. While there are often classes that teach computer programs at continuing education departments of local schools, you can learn much by reading the manual. I find such manuals intimidating, so I never try to absorb the complete manual in one session or even two or three. I block out sections of the manual to learn over a month.

RE-WRITE

When you have finished your book and you have pages of manuscript, plunge into the three Rs: re-read, revise and re-write. It is tempting to send your manuscript away as a finished product. You feel as though you've finished it. You feel a sense of accomplishment and completion, but now is the time to make it more polished, more readable, more professional. Try to get the manuscript in good order. Try to have it exactly as you want it. If some part of it bothers you, take the time to change it. Your intuition is probably right and you might as well change it now as later.

Ask yourself if you adequately fulfilled your book outline? Is your information complete? Did you maintain the same style throughout? the same tone? If you wrote a chapter in a serious, didactic style, did you write the next chapter in a chatty, breezy style? Try to be consistent. Are your sentences as clear as they can be? Use a good English grammar text for more information.

Don't say	When you can say
by virtue of the fact that	because
in the event of	if
could of	could have
should of	should have
all of	all
all of a sudden	suddenly
quite a few	some
irregardless	regardless

Check your manuscript for the overuse of a favourite word. In every manuscript I overuse a different word. In one book it was "easily". In this book I had to ruthlessly weed out "information".

There does come a time when you are so sick of reading your manuscript that you can't tell if any of it is adequate. That is when you give the manuscript to, at least, two readers.

READ FOR CONTENT

Choose readers who are knowledgeable in the field. If you are writing non-fiction, this is particularly important. If you are writing fiction, choose readers who read a lot of fiction. These are friends who are not paid for their work. Ask them to tell you what parts they liked about it, what they found confusing or unclear, what they found boring. Don't expect a written response, but try to spend time with your reader and talk about the book. Make notes of what they tell you. Don't argue with them. If you do, they will stop talking and you will never know what valuable advice they could have offered. You may not accept their advice, but thank them for it and write it down. Don't rush to your manuscript and immediately write in the changes suggested and don't screw up the notes you made and

27

throw them in the wastebasket. Think about them for a day. At first you may reject all the changes suggested, but reflection usually gives you a better perspective on the problems. After a day or two, you can approach your manuscript to improve it.

EDIT

The best way to find an editor is to check in the Editors' Association of Canada directory in the library. The directory lists telephone numbers as well as their "hot line" for advice. Editors are listed in this directory with their experience and their areas of expertise. As well, you can phone small publishing houses and ask if they use free-lance editors and if they would recommend one to you. Get several names. Phone the free-lance editors and ask what books they have previously edited, then read the books. Decide on an editor and ask her rates. You can either ask for an estimate on the work after she has seen the manuscript or ask for a contract price. Editors usually work at an hourly rate, but the cost of editing your manuscript can vary greatly. Make a clear agreement with your editor so there are no surprises when you get your bill. Do you want the editor to read your manuscript and advise you on its content? structure? literary merit? Do you want your grammar corrected? spelling and punctuation corrected? You want this editor to give you advice on the strong points of the manuscript as well as the weak points. You want ideas. "Your heroine's actions aren't consistent in Paragraph 4, Chapter 8." "Your information on mushrooms while accurate seems dull." Usually, you are less interested in your editor's ability to spot small errors, since many people with less qualifications can pick up your spelling and grammar mistakes. However, keep in mind that such errors scream at a competent editor and it is almost impossible for her or him not to automatically mark them. It's an editorial reflex action.

The Writers' Union of Canada offers a manuscript evaluation service which gives written comments on the content and writing technique of your manuscript. At the time of this writing the fees were $125 plus GST for a ten page submission, $125 for first ten pages and $2 per page plus GST for a full manuscript. Their address is at the back of the book.

It is important to realize that a reader who can spot grammar and typing mistakes is not "editing" your work; he is "proof-reading" it. You need someone to edit who can advise you on concepts, plot, meaning, characters, organization and style.

Editors usually are specialists. An editor may be a fiction editor, or a non-fiction editor, an expert on histories or on "how-to" books. Ask what books the editor has recently worked on and find one whose subject competence matches your book.

A good editor will not change your style. She will support it, enhance it and make your manuscript clearer, more concise and more readable. Try not to get upset by criticism. The editor is probably right, not necessarily, but probably. Put your emotional reaction to her comments aside and work on the manuscript.

RE-WRITE

When you receive the manuscript from the editor, with her comments on the pages, and usually a long (as many as sixteen pages) letter, pay her bill. Then think for days about what advice she has given. Re-write. I usually do this re-write in pen on top of my old manuscript. When I have done all the re-writes in the book, I type the corrections onto my computer copy and print it.

It doesn't matter how you do it, but this editing process is the most important work you can do to move your book into the professional arena.

You have hired an editor who works in the commercial book industry. She knows what will make your book tighter, more interesting, more believable. If you don't trust her advice, hire a different editor. Your editor is going to make the greatest single difference in the quality of your book.

PROOFREAD

When you have incorporated all the suggestions you can into your manuscript, re-form it, re-print it or re-type it and give a copy of the book to two friends for proofreading. These can be relatives, biased cheerleaders of your work, members of your family. You want someone who will read every word and pick up mistakes. If you are working on a word processor, you have already put the chapters through an automatic spelling corrector (available in software and invaluable). However, the spell check doesn't know the difference between the correct use of "two" and "to," and some spell checks are better than others, so you may still have errors. Ask your proofreaders to work slowly and carefully and mark the errors on the manuscript. They don't need to write the corrections. It helps if they put a mark in the margin also, so you don't miss any errors. There are always errors in a book. If you are working on a typewriter and have to have your manuscript transcribed to disk, the typist will make errors that you will have to catch.

If you send your disk to a printer, then only your errors should be transcribed. However, this isn't always true. "Computer garbage" can sneak onto your disk and onto the hard copy. Coding problems can put wrong headings in the wrong place, indentations in the wrong place or italics where you didn't want them. Chapters can be in the wrong order. Paragraphs can be out of sequence, or swallowed into some computer black hole and missing completely. Convinced? You must read your proofs. If the mistakes are the printer's, he or she will rectify the mistakes without charge, but you must find them. Try to correct every one, because there are sure to be mistakes that you and the proofreaders have missed.

Now you are ready to produce the book.

PART THREE:
Getting Published

Marion Crook

3

How to Get Published

LOOKING FOR A PUBLISHER

If, after producing the manuscript, you realize that you don't want
to publish it yourself—you don't have the time, energy or money
it takes to get the book into print—you may decide to look for a
publisher. This is a skill in itself. Brilliant ideas may not reach print
if they are poorly presented. Publishers rarely read more than the
first page of a proposal. That first page tells the publisher how well
you write. A good presentation is very important.

Search the shelves of your local book store for publishers who
have published books that are similar to yours. If you have already
done this, you will have a list. Check that list against a writer's
handbook such as *The Canadian Writer's Guide* or *Canadian
Markets for Writers and Photographers* and find the name of the
contact person and the current address of the publishing firm.
Prepare your materials (see following pages) and send to several
(perhaps five) publishers at the same time. Check in the writers'
handbooks to see if the publisher states that they will not accept
multiple submissions. If they don't state that, you may send your
manuscript to several publishing houses at the same time. If you get
more than one offer, celebrate; that would be wonderful! With two
offers, you could ask advice of the Writers' Union.

Expectations

You may look on a publisher as a great protector, someone who will do all the work and make you rich and famous—the kindly benefactor of fantasy who will look after you. It doesn't happen like that. Although a publisher is often better placed in the industry than you are to assess the market, produce and promote the book, you still will have to do a great deal of work to get the manuscript ready, provide lists of potential markets as well as write promotional material. You still have to pay for your own publicity photographs, pay for indexing (if your book requires it) and, other than the six to ten free copies you receive at printing, buy your own copies, usually at a discount. If you are a good business person, you will stay alert for promotional and sales opportunities and will have a working relationship with the staff of the publishing house. Publishers want authors who can produce, promote and sell.

Big or Small

Should you send your manuscript to a big publishing house or a small one? A big one might have a greater advertising budget and a larger distribution system. On the other hand, it will have more books to promote and it might not put that big budget behind your book. A smaller company might make fewer sales, but give you more control over the book and promote it more readily. Look through the book shelves of your, by now familiar, book store for samples of books published by the company that interests you. Read the publisher's catalogues for a greater understanding of their publishing program. Don't send your manuscript of poetry to a publisher of business books. It is surprising how often authors approach a publisher without investigating the kind of book the publisher produces. I once received a very long handwritten manuscript of philosophy. I published mysteries. Try to tailor your presentation to the needs of the company you approach. They usually have a well defined section of the market that they serve. You should note past and recent publications to see if the publishing house has made changes in their publishing focus. Whether you approach Random House in Toronto or Orca Books in Victoria, you need to use a professional approach.

The Query Letter

I used to recommend Michael Larson's book *How to Write A Query Letter* but it was such a popular book that it disappeared from my local library. It is no longer listed in *Books in Print*, so it is probably not available, but there are others. Check your bookstore and your library.

In your query letter to a publisher, try to give a description of your book in one sentence. Publishers want to understand your request as quickly as possible. Write: "This book describes the migration of the disease-carrying rat into our urban areas." or "This book shows the horrific effects of the unforgiving sea on the life of an Irish community." or "This book allows teens to speak out about why they try suicide in such great numbers." You will find writing a one-sentence description surprisingly hard to do, but it is necessary. Until you can put the general theme of the book into one sentence, it may be impossible to interest anyone in it. I sometimes imagine that I am writing ad copy for the book. What can I say that will describe it fairly and yet entice someone to buy it? That kind of advertising description will interest a publisher. Include this information in a one page business letter.

As well, you need to include a one-page synopsis. For fiction, that would be a brief plot outline, for non-fiction, the direction and general theme of the book and a chapter outline with a short paragraph about each chapter. Non-fiction also requires some information about how your book is better than the books already on the market on this subject. In other words, why should the publisher buy it?

Also, you need to include a list of your accomplishments, particularly a list of your published works. If you have never published before, give a reason why you are the one who should write the book—you have studied the rats in the garbage cans of the city for two years; you have interviewed the inhabitants of four Irish coastal villages and have a degree in anthropology—whatever makes your information credible.

If you have any reviews of previous work (and they are favourable) include them. Be sure you date the review and cite the source. Recent reviews published within the past two years are more impressive than aging ones.

The Professional Approach

Make your presentation to the publisher look professional—no hand-written notes on yellow note pads, no hastily-typed, faded, dot-matrix copy full of typing and spelling errors. Try to produce your material and your letter on clean, neatly typed, white paper. Include a self-addressed stamped envelope for an answer. If you don't need the accompanying material returned and just want an answer from the publisher, say that at the bottom of your letter. If you send material to an American publisher, include either an international reply coupon or some American stamps. Do not staple any material; use paper clips if necessary.

Waiting

Then find something to occupy your anxieties while you wait for an answer. Check your resource books for writers; the reply time is often stated in them. If no time is stated, wait two months. You may then phone or write and ask for an answer. There is no point in demanding a response. Publishers have told me stories of authors who have yelled at them over the phone and insisted on a reply. This gets them a quick answer in the negative. Be persistent, but polite, systematic and patient. Keep track of where you send your inquiries, to whom and when. Keep copies of all your letters.

Vanity Press

You do have the choice of sending your manuscript to a vanity press. A vanity press accepts your money and produces a book. It does not depend on the sale of that book to make money; it takes its profit from the author. You have no control over the print, the cover or the marketing. Editing is limited to a cursory look for obscenities or libelous statements which could land the publishers in court. A vanity press will not pay an editor to improve the quality of writing since its profits do not depend on sales. They may suggest that you, the author pay an editor, but they will not take on that cost. They can charge from $5,000 to $40,000 to produce your book. Vanity press books are seldom accepted by booksellers or the library trade. They are not considered a commercial enterprise. But they do print your name on the book.

GETTING A CONTRACT

If you are offered a legitimate contract by a publishing company and have no idea whether the offer is excellent or insulting, you may want to check with the Writers' Union of Canada. They offer contract advice of various sorts. One offer is a collection of pamphlets for a modest $18. Another is a written evaluation for a fee of $200 plus GST. If you wish the Writers' Union representative to negotiate the contract for you, the fee is $600 plus GST (for non-members of the Union).

Generally, you will need to pay attention to the advance offered by the publisher. Canadian publishers do not offer big advances. From the writer's point of view, they do not even offer "reasonable" advances. While a few authors command advances of $10,000 or more, most writers take $500, $1,000 to $3,000.

Royalties are calculated on the retail price and sometimes on the net price. There is a big difference. They range from 6% to 10% with royalties of half that on discounted books. Some publishers offer percentage increments of 10%, 12 1/2% and 15% at, perhaps, 5,000, 10,000 and 15,000 volume sales. You can sometimes bargain a decreased advance for an increased increment.

There are many rights and licenses that are included in a contract: (a) digest, newspaper, periodical and book condensation rights (b) foreign rights (c) reprint in other works (d) Book Club rights (e) film broadcasting, television and sound broadcasting rights (f) translation rights (g) unbound sheets (h) direct mail rights (i) extracts of the book (j) serial rights (k) other, such as future technology (l) multimedia rights and (m) moral rights.

While much could be said about each category, I will discuss only the two which seem to cause the most difficulty: multimedia rights and moral rights.

Contracts license multimedia rights. This is a difficult section of the contract since it is hard to know what kind of sales the publisher will make. Publishers offer everything from 10% to 75% here. Sometimes this section can be written to include film rights, but 50% for film rights is low and 10% is unthinkable. You need to protect your rights. You also should not license unknown future technology (there is usually a clause in the contract about all future technologies) since you don't know what they would be or how much they would be worth.

Some publishers ask you to waive your moral rights. The Writer's Union tells you never to sign away your moral rights because then you would not control the way in which others use your work. Publishers say they can't sell film rights if the author retains moral rights. You need to find a way to deal with this difficult dilemma. Some publishers do not insist on this; some do.

Read your contract and try to imagine how it will affect you. Remember that the contract is an offer which you can negotiate. It is usual to counter offer and ask for some changes. Once you sign the contract, do not complain about the terms to other authors. Also, do not brag about the terms you received. If you have negotiated a particularly good contract and you tell the world about it, you put the publisher in the position of having to explain to other authors why their contract is not as good as yours. You will be unlikely to get such good terms again.

You are responsible for the veracity of your research. If you write libel, you can be sued. While publishers welcome controversy as it sells books, no one wants a libel action. Be credible and responsible. If you have a quote, get the legal permission to use it from the person you quote. Don't use the name of those you interview without their permission. More about this later.

You may be vitally interested in how many books the publisher is going to print in the initial press run. In my experience, publishers seldom tell you this, at least, not when they are negotiating the contract. They must consider many aspects of sales when they decide upon the print run, one of which is the advance sales of the book. Until they have a contract with you, they won't make advance sales. At least, they seldom do. I did work with one publisher who was so sure we would come to an agreement that the company advertised my book in its catalogue before I had signed the contract.

If you send out your book to a publisher in hopes of getting a contract and the publisher replies indicating interest and makes suggestions while rejecting your manuscript, consider the response as free editorial advice and pay attention. You may use these ideas to sell your manuscript to someone else. Selling your manuscript is usually a process, not a one-shot event, and it often takes reflection, readjustment and repeated efforts.

PART FOUR:
Planning
for Production

Marion Crook

Planning Ahead 4

If you decide that you will not offer your book to a publisher, or you have been rejected by several publishers for reasons other than poor writing and you decide that you will self publish your book, read the following attentively.

PLANNING
The Mental Adjustment

After your manuscript is in perfect order, after you have used creativity and energy to produce a good manuscript, turn off the writer part of your personality and become a business person. Look on the manuscript as a product, something you have to deliver to the public as efficiently as possible. You may view this publishing project as the beginning of a long series of publishing works or you may view it as a one-time project the way you would a new boat or a holiday, a pleasurable way to spend your indulgence money. If it is your intention to publish only this one book, there is no reason it can't be the best book possible. It is a labour of love and an exciting investment of your time and talents, so whether this is going to be the only book you publish or one of many, you still need to make it the best product possible.

Those of us who want to publish and continue to publish view publishing as a business. We have a business person's need to define goals, keep accurate records, establish credibility in the industry and make a profit. All our goals must take into consideration: how the book will look, how it will be used and how well it will sell. Those attributes must all relate to what the consumer wants, and what we want.

The Business Plan

Most companies have a business plan: some detailed, some in computer spread sheets, some in a corner of the owner's mind. With the exception of a rare genius who has a calculator in his head, the more care you use to write your business plan, the more organized, efficient and effective you will be in carrying out that plan.

Industry Canada discusses a business plan on their website at *strategis.ic.gc.ca.* If you are not on-line, check the federal and provincial business service centres in cities across Canada. They provide much information for start-up businesses and can give you brochures and counselling. I also recommend Frances McGuckin's *Business for Beginners* which covers much of what you need to know to start a business.

A business plan includes a financial plan and more. It includes a review of the company's efforts to date, the aims of the company for the next year and the next five years, the personnel needed to carry out the plans, the promotion and advertising needed, how the company plans to use agents and distributors, and the marketing objectives and strategies. Many small colleges offer help with this. If you have worked out a business plan, you may get constructive criticism from your accountant or a friend who already runs a small business. Some provinces have a Ministry of Industry and Small Business that offers sample business plans and literature on various aspects of business planning. In BC, the Department of Small Business, Tourism and Culture has a resource library that contains a great deal of practical information. In Vancouver, this is contained in the library at the Canada-BC Business Service Centre. In other areas of Canada, Community Futures offices will have similar information. Check in your phone book for resources in your area.

Accountants

Use your accountant as a source of information. Read your business plan, write down the questions you want to ask and, before you start your business, talk to your accountant asking for the most efficient way to work. The accountant's advice will shape your business ventures. Her advice should take into consideration your sources of income and your expenses and should be specific to your financial status. One person may find an incorporated company the most efficient vehicle for his publishing company while another may find it advantageous not to incorporate.

If your publishing business is personal, that is, not an incorporated company, and the expenses of the business are part of your overall income (or liability), you can use your decreased taxes as an asset. Ask your accountant if the publishing business will result in lower taxes.

FINANCING
Banks

If you need financing for your book publishing, your ability to get it depends on the value of your present assets. Bankers seldom are willing to finance such speculative projects as books in a consignment-based industry. If you have a past record with your bank of starting profitable businesses and you have sufficient income or assets to cover your loan, you will probably have little trouble getting money at reasonable rates. Bankers usually are not interested in taking inventory as collateral although some banks allow you to claim inventory as collateral at the remainder value. (Probably about one quarter the cost of production.) You would need some proof that a remainder company would buy your unsold stock before any loans officer at a bank would consider it saleable. In today's economic climate, such collateral is viewed by bankers as extremely risky. You really do not want to go into business with the idea that you are going to lose money, but bankers are interested in the worst thing that could happen. While you need the detailed information on how the banker could recover his money if you sold no books at all, your attitude to your business should be a good deal more positive—or don't publish.

Approaching the Bank

By the time you approach the bank, you have a reasonable idea of where your market is and how many books you can expect to sell. Prepare a financial evaluation sheet for the banker and enclose copies of the production costs from three printers. Estimate all your expenses including office overhead, telephone, vehicle costs and postage. Bring with you any advance orders, any indications of interest by big groups. (If the International Mushroom Growers of North America wrote you a letter saying that they could hardly wait for your book since it represented the last unexplored area for mushrooms in the country and they would like you to speak at their national conference, bring the letter with your financial statement.) Your repayment plan to the bank must be reasonable and foreseeable. You should show a selling price between four and five times the production costs in order to pay your expenses and create a small profit. Remember that distribution companies charge between 55% and 65% to distribute your book.

When you approach a banker or any other investor be confident. Banks are interested in your assets: your house, your car, your horse and your stamp collection. Have with you a list of your assets with their values. The bank will be unlikely to lend money on the promise of future sales unless you have a firm corporate sale and, even then, a banker will prefer solid assets.

Have as much information as you can assemble ready when you approach the bank. Know exactly how much money you need by what dates. Know what interest rates you would like to have and give the banker some re-payment schedule. Be business like. Be organized. Be practical.

Private Loans

The cheapest way to get a loan is usually from the bank. However, for 500 copies of a 32 page book, you might be able to get better terms from your mother. Explore all possibilities. Printers used to reluctantly finance the printing of books in some cases. This rarely happens today. Printers will simply hold the shipment of books until paid in full. By paying promptly for your first edition, you may secure some credit privileges from the printer in the future.

INCOME TAX

Get a receipt for everything you spend and save all of them. Any expenses that are incurred on behalf of your book are expenses of your business. It is surprising how they mount up in a year. You may claim a portion of your house rent and heat and hydro expenses as office expenses on your book, but you have to remember that, should you sell your house, this small portion of your house—it might be 1/20th of the area of your house—is subject to tax on any excess of the selling price over your purchase price. If you rent an apartment and use a separate room as an office, you can claim part of your rent as office expense. These stipulations change as the Income Tax Act and the interpretation of it changes. You need to get recent, professional, tax accounting advice.

You probably can claim a portion of your vehicle expenses provided you use your vehicle in the business of producing or selling the book. If you claim your vehicle as a business expense, remember to put business-use insurance on it. If you do not, you may be denied coverage if you have an accident. You may be allowed to use your car for business a certain number of hours a month without business insurance, so check with your company.

FANTASYLAND

Do not print your book expecting a market to develop once the book is available. Discover the extent of your market before you print. It is both financially and emotionally rewarding to sell out a printing. Therefore, do not make the printing so big that you are left, after your market is exhausted, with thousands of unsaleable books stacked in your basement. My first book of fiction *A Yen For Trouble* sold three thousand five hundred copies. This is a respectable number in the Canadian trade fiction market. Unfortunately, I did not research the market when I printed it and did an initial run of five thousand. If I'd produced an initial run of two thousand and paid interest only on that cost, sold out, re-financed, re-printed one thousand, sold out, re-financed, re-printed another one thousand, I would have been left with only five hundred books to write off instead of fifteen hundred and would have avoided big interest costs. Consider my experience the result of lack of knowledge, and be forewarned. You don't need to repeat my mistake.

CO-PUBLISHING

It is possible to co-author and co-publish as Nancy and I are doing with this book. It is also possible to co-publish with someone other than another author. We published this book under a joint venture agreement—two authors and two publishers. You could investigate co-publishing your book on salmon hatcheries with the Atlantic Fish Farmers Association (assuming there is one). Books on mountaineering could be co-published with a climbing or outdoors club. Cookbooks could be co-published with a local or national charitable organization. Writers groups could co-publish an anthology. A small publishing company could produce a book and contract with a larger company for distribution and sales. It is also possible for small presses to band together in order to apply for funding from the Department of Culture. Such funding would not be available to one press, but may be available to a co-operative publishing project.

In the same way, a small press might gain funding if it co-operatively publishes with a much larger firm. If you take your book and enter into an agreement with a larger company, you may give up control of your book while you gain sales. The larger company may agree to sell your book under its distribution system only if the cover is changed to suit them, the imprint is the bigger company's and the content is edited by their editors. Investigate your options. The agreement between the parties must be clear so that each publisher knows who has which responsibility.

In group or co-publishing it is wise to have a lawyer (one who is familiar with the law of intellectual property) discuss your needs with you and draw up a legal agreement. If you prepare a written statement of a tentative agreement before you go to a lawyer, your legal costs will be much less than if you walk into her office and ask her to think out the problems for you. She should look at your tentative agreement, add, subtract and adjust information, and then give you a contract. The problems of proceeding without a contract are not so much that your partners will try to take more than their share of profit or do less than their share of work so much as they will forget what they agreed to in the first place and make assumptions that are new to you. A legal agreement also assures that money will be available when promised and removes much of the worry of being left to pay the printer's bill alone.

46

NON-PROFIT SOCIETIES

Books are produced by groups who use the proceeds of the sales to help their causes such as women's institutes, religious groups and historical societies. The principal problem with such productions is the lack of editing. You can tell them, and repeat it and emphasize it, but when the contributions to the book come in, somehow the need for editing is ignored. The president, regardless of his talent, is often expected to edit the manuscript. He shouldn't do it. The editor of a group publication must be ruthless in excluding inappropriate contributions. This is too much to ask of a volunteer editor who is a member of the group. Hire an editor. It is obvious when you don't.

One of the advantages of producing a book with a non-profit society is well-organized, free distribution; everyone becomes an uncommissioned salesperson. Usually such a society has a membership list that can serve as a direct mail vehicle. Such societies often have affiliations with other groups who have additional membership lists of people who are interested in the subject matter of the book. The organization may have secretarial services that you can use. Society members may also pre-order the book with an accomanying cheque before publication reducing the financial risk of the publisher. Consumers are also inclined to purchase a book in support of the cause of the society. How many of us own a cookbook published by a community group?

Producing a book can be an exciting project for a group giving interest and pleasure to many and resulting in a collective pride in the final result. But a good product usually depends on the advice of an outside editor, and a committee who stands behind that editor's decisions.

Non-profit societies can also hire authors to write a complete book for them, often on a flat contract, no royalties basis. The fees vary, but may be calculated on an hourly rate times the number of hours the author estimates he or she will need to write the book. (Be clear in advance about who will own the copyright to the work when complete.) Even when the book is professionally written, the committee in charge of the book must still hire an outside editor. I can't repeat "Hire an editor"often enough. An editor makes your book more professional, more acceptable in the industry and usually more profitable.

47

PROFIT

How much profit can you expect? Your profit is dependent on the cost of production, your selling price and the number of sales you make. Markets have a resistance to prices beyond a certain amount. A quick look at other books on your subject will tell you the price range. While Nancy will discuss the way in which you price a book, I want you to consider here that it's unlikely that you or a publisher of your work could afford to publish a book with no hope of profit. You need to look at your market.

Consumers will buy an instructional book more readily than a book of fiction, principally, I would guess, because an instructional book is useful and a book of fiction or poetry is pleasurable and therefore an indulgence. The competition in your area as well as the public's attitude to spending limit your price setting. Very often, your only control on profit is to keep your expenses low.

Your expenses include printing, art work, editing, mailing, postage, telephone, legal fees and, for some, a percentage to a distributor. You must balance your costs and profit against your projected income before you publish. How many books do you need to sell in order to get your costs paid? How soon can you reasonably expect to accomplish that? Publishing is a fascinating business and can seduce you to spend money. You need to remember to plan for profit.

While a publisher is looking for profit, he views his product differently than does a producer of can-openers. Publishers have faith; publishers have dreams; publishers believe in luck. And some publishers who have a great feeling of social responsibility to a cause or to an art have a compulsion to publish. Their motive for publishing is not necessarily financial gain, but they recognize that few can continue to publish without balancing costs with sales.

It is important to look at where your passion for publishing lies, in what book, and then work out whether you can make a profit publishing that particular book. It may be that you can make a profit on a different book which could pay for the production of the book you want to publish, but which you know will not make big sales. Do your projections and costing ahead of time so you are not surprised by your profit or your potential losses.

BOOK PUBLISHERS AND THE LAW
Copyright

In Canada the author automatically owns the copyright to her work unless the author works for a government or a company that expects such work as part of the job. If you do nothing—do not register the copyright in any way—but simply write the material and put your name on it, you still own the copyright in Canada, the United States, Britain and countries which abide by the International Copyright Convention. If you are not a citizen of Canada or of one of the countries covered by the Convention, check with a lawyer for the status of your copyright.

To further protect your copyright, you can also mail your manuscript to yourself under registered mail. Do not open the package when it arrives back to you. Use the registration receipt as proof that you did indeed write this manuscript before the date of the postal registration. This is not as useful as registering your copyright officially, but it may be better than no record at all.

You can officially register the copyright so that you have a document to produce in court if there is any question of ownership. To register a copyright send a fee ($65 as of October 1999) to Canadian Intellectual Property Office, Industry Canada, Copyright and Industrial Design Branch, Tower #1, 50 Victoria St., Place du Portage, Hull, Quebec, K1A 0C9. It is not necessary to send along a copy of the book. Some lawyers advise that you do send a copy of the book to the copyright office even if the office refuses to accept it, but the advice from the Copyright office is: please, don't send us your book.

The content of your book becomes a property and, as such, the rights to it can be sold, assigned or licensed for use. Do not sell your copyright. It is a whole basket of rights and licenses. You can sell many of the rights to your book, while retaining your copyright. Canadian publishers don't ask you for your copyright, at least legitimate publishers don't, so this seldom arises. If you sell your copyright, you have no more rights to the work.

When you sell rights to your book, you sell the publisher the right to use your work. The contract contains provisions for those rights to revert to you should the publisher fail to comply with the terms of the sale. You could also sell only some rights to your book.

You could retain, for instance, the film rights or foreign rights.

When you assign the rights of your book, you usually transfer them legally to some other person or some other company and you no longer have any control over your work. You will have been paid for this or you may have given them as a gift.

When you grant a licence to your book for a fee, you allow a company the use of your work to a specified user for a specified period of time, for instance in a radio broadcast, or for one magazine edition. After an agreed period, the rights revert to you. Selling separate licenses to various parts of your book may be a good way to make money on your book as well as a way to increase publicity.

Liability

As the owner of the book, you are responsible for what is printed in it. You are responsible for accuracy, fairness of the content and that no one is libelled. You can buy liability insurance, but most small presses do not carry any. They rely on their editing judgement to carefully screen out anything that could be construed as defamatory or libelous.

Permissions

Be sure to obtain written permission from anyone who contributes to your book. Ask, in a letter, for the right to quote them, or reproduce a specific piece of work (describe it) in your book and have them sign such a permission. Obtain that permission before the book is printed so that you can choose to delete that section of the book if they refuse to grant permission or ask too much money for the privilege. It is difficult to negotiate a permission after the book is on the bookseller's shelves.

Lawyers

After you have drawn up a business plan for your company and one for the book you plan to produce, read the plan thoroughly and mark any section where you question the law. What do you do about outstanding debts over ninety days? What is the effect on your heirs if you die before the book is produced and only have debts to leave them? What happens to you if the printer adds an additional cost to the book? What happens to your cost of produc-

50

tion if the printer does not fulfil on time? makes an error on the cover? loses the original art work? The printer neglected to print the back cover of *Not Quite Alone*. I discovered the omission in the lawyer's office. Luckily, the printer was a reputable one and insisted on recalling the books and replacing the covers at his expense. These things do happen. When you have read your plan and written notes to yourself on the parts that you question, make a list of the questions, make a copy of the business plan and take both to a lawyer.

Choose a lawyer who has a solid background in business law. Lawyers vary in competence and experience. Ask a prosperous business person whom she uses as a lawyer. Let your friends know that you are looking for legal advice and collect references. When you make an appointment with a lawyer ask for a rough estimate of the cost of consultation. This small piece of advice is one I neglected when Nancy and I were pursuing a company who had admired the first edition of this book so much they plagiarized it. We did manage to stop their production and force the destruction of their existing books as well as obtain an apology to us in their company newsletter, but I forgot to ask the lawyer what his charges would be and found that after a few months, we collected four thousand dollars in compensation from the company only to hand over all the money plus $1,600 to the lawyer in fees. I should take my own advice!

Your first consultation with the lawyer should answer questions that will never need to be asked again. Ask the lawyer how you should set up your business. Is it a proprietorship? a partnership? a company? How do your expenses, losses or profits affect your income tax? If you are borrowing money for this book, what type of security should you be prepared to offer and what is your liability if repayment is not as you had expected? After this appointment, any questions you have concerning legal problems could probably be dealt with on the telephone at less cost. You should leave the lawyers office after that first visit feeling as though you understand the legal implications of your decisions. If the lawyer you choose does not understand the publishing business, ask him or her to find out the information and call you back; or find a lawyer who does.

Try to organize your business plans so that the time you spend with a lawyer and an accountant is brief and relatively inexpensive.

51

Use this advice to protect yourself. Do not be so enthusiastic about your book project that you neglect to look after yourself. Ask your lawyer and your accountant what can happen to you financially if your worst fears are realized—and then work hard to see that such calamities never happen.

Keep an image in your mind of the end product, the real book that you can pick off a shelf and open, running your hand over the smooth pages, smelling the clean ink and congratulating yourself on a difficult job well done. You can make it happen.

PART FIVE:
Publishing the Manuscript

Nancy Wise

Producing a Book 5

Few people outside of the book industry are aware of the amount of planning and work required to create a finished book. Writing a book is often just the first step. For every hour of writing, there can be a corresponding hour of production work. Producing a book by yourself means that you are responsible for the appearance of your final product. You must assume all of the functions of a commercial publisher with one great disadvantage: lack of experience. Don't let this discourage you. You will learn as you go along. Many commercial publishers began their careers as self publishers. The lessons they learned with their first books helped them when they went on to their second ones. Almost every publisher has a story about pages incorrectly numbered, pages missed altogether or covers that scuffed with the gentlest touch. Producing a book is a creative challenge with an end reward of personal accomplishment and potential cash profits.

DESKTOP PUBLISHING

The technological changes that have taken place in publishing since this book first appeared are astounding. With the advent of desktop publishing, page composition is now performed in a paperless environment on the screen of your computer monitor. *Text* and *graphics manipulation* are terms that have generally replaced paste up and copyfitting by hand. Using a mouse or keyboard commands on the computer, it is now possible in seconds to move or reposition blocks of text, sentences or single words. Formatting the size of type for headings, sub-headings or body text is a simple matter of highlighting and selecting fonts, sizes and styles (for **boldface**, *italic* or normal type). With such powerful publishing programs as *Ventura*, *QuarkXPress* and *PageMaker* available in the $500 to $800 range, most of the production tasks once done by hand can be performed directly on home computers to produce printer-ready pages or disk copies. Less powerful programs are also available for under $200, but the lower end of the range of software tends to lack finesse or the capabilities to manage precise text placement or graphics enhancement.

Compatibility

Compatibility relates to the ability of one software program to communicate with a different software program. Compatibility also relates to computer systems. The major personal computer systems are *Apple Macintosh* and *IBM*, and also include IBM compatible *MS-DOS* and *Windows*. Marion and I have computers with IBM compatible systems. Our software differs (I use *Microsoft Word*; Marion uses *WordPerfect*) but we can still exchange copy on disk and load each other's work into our respective programs because our software and computer systems are compatible. The problem I initially ran into in producing this edition was that PageMaker, the publishing program I use, is an older version than my word processing program. PageMaker would not import or accept what I had already written in MS Word. I was able to avoid disaster (having to re-type the manuscript) by saving the Word version to an ASCII file, a computer "language" that my PageMaker version could accept.

I've related this near disaster to make the point that you should check the compatibility of your software before you start writing and keep your software upgraded to within a few versions of what is currently on the market. If you have a publishing program, make sure it will import data from your word processing software. If you don't have a publishing software program, check with local desktop publishing companies and various book printers to see if their computer systems will accept your word processing program. Look for companies that are able to convert IBM files to MacIntosh files if necessary. By asking some preliminary questions in advance, you'll rest easier as your production work progresses. It is a rude surprise to discover no one can use or convert your disk files.

Writing to Disk

Force yourself to learn to write on a computer keyboard. Do whatever you have to do to get your manuscript on a computer disk. I confess to handwriting parts of this in hotel rooms while on a sales trip. I don't own a laptop computer and was happy to resort to pen and paper in complete isolation. Having to re-type my handwriting later, however, reinforced the appeal of creating the manuscript on computer. There are so many advantages. Time is a huge factor, as are the cost savings once you have your manuscript on disk. You don't have to pay anyone to type for you. Editing or adding to the text is simple and quick. Determining your format, doing your layout, deciding the number of pages are a breeze compared to the laborious and sometimes heroic tasks required prior to the affordability of consumer oriented computers. By having your manuscript on disk, you will save money when working with a book printer. It's difficult to think of any disadvantages other than the initial cost in both money and time to set up and learn the software. While computers make publishing simpler and more cost effective, you won't catch me saying it's always easier. Doing layout on a computer is a huge and often tedious job that requires the same attention to detail as manual paste up. Computer production is simpler, but it's still work.

If you don't own a computer, but you've finished re-typing your edited manuscript for the tenth time and you really *want* to publish electronically, don't despair. There are a couple of options. You can pay someone to re-type it on a computer and have them give you a copy on disk, or you can go to a desktop publishing company and have them scan your manuscript instead.

Desktop Publishing Companies

No one said you have to perform all of the production work yourself. The demand for computer publishing services is reflected in the number of desktop publishing companies now in business. These companies can do almost everything required to bring your manuscript to the printer-ready stage. If you have a manuscript that you lovingly plunked out on your manual typewriter, a desktop publishing firm can help you. Using sophisticated software and equipment, they can scan your typewritten pages into a computer using an OCR (Optical Character Recognition) program such as *WordScan*. Once scanned, the file can be saved as a word processing file, copied to disk and there you are—all set to get on with producing your book. (As simple as this sounds, your original manuscript must be typed using a crisp, new ribbon and without handwritten comments or corrections for the computer to convert the typed letters. Even so, you must very carefully proofread scanned files to catch any inexact translations that can occur in the process.) Be sure to get clear quotes in advance on what work will be performed, how the company charges (hourly or flat fee) and what constitutes additional charges. You'll find desktop companies in your local telephone book. It's always best to get quotes from various companies before committing to any one.

Book Producers

There are companies and individuals that offer all-inclusive production services. A book producer will take your material, prepare it for the printer, make arrangements for the printing, and return to you a finished, printed book. They often charge a flat fee or may submit specific bills to you for payment for the various aspects of editing, production and printing. Do not mistake these companies for vanity press publishing companies which generally put their imprint on the book and claim ownership. With book producers, once you pay them for their services, you retain your rights as a publisher. Dealing with a book production company is like having a general contractor when building a house. The production company will consult with you, deal with the subtrades (an editor, designers, printers) on your behalf and produce your book according to the standards expected by the book industry. It is certainly an easier option if you have no interest in learning how to publish and are willing to pay to have someone do all the work for you. Some desktop publishing companies will perform the same services. Professional book printers also offer in-house production services. Investigate your best cost options.

Computers and Self Publishing

Computers provide the means by which almost anyone can produce printed pages at home and have them turned into a book by a printer. However, some people publish without an awareness of or respect for the standards required by the general book industry. Poorly produced books promoted by overzealous authors have contributed to a stigma that reflects badly on every self publisher. Having the desire and the technology to produce books is not enough. Know when to hire outside help in preparing your book for the printer. Use your computer's capabilities with responsibility and understand your limitations. Decide what you can do and what should be contracted out in order to produce the best book possible. Understanding the production and printing process will help you make these decisions.

CHOOSING A BOOK FORMAT

Defining the format and determining the length of your book are two basic elements that must be established very early in the publishing process.

Let's assume that you don't own a publishing program but you do have a computer with a word processing program. You've done some market research prior to writing, your manuscript has been professionally edited and is now a reasonable length for a first book venture. By reasonable, I mean a manuscript that can be published at a cost that will result in a fair retail price. If you write on computer as I usually do, it's easy to ramble on long past the time when your point has been made. I rely on our editor to trim out extraneous prose, and I do not believe every word I write must be published. Listen to your editor and weigh the importance of a paragraph or a chapter against the costs of including it in your book. I have seen unedited, self published novels thicker than a metro telephone book and hopelessly overpriced for today's retail market. Remember to be

59

strict with yourself and be guided by quality rather than quantity.

You need to know in advance how long your book will be when you publish your finished manuscript. To make this decision, you must decide on a book size. It should be no surprise that there are standard sizes in the book industry ranging from 8.5 x 11 inch books to those that measure 6 x 9 inches and 5.5 by 8.5 inches. These sizes are not arbitrary, but relate to the best economies derived from the bulk press sheets used by printers. You can make some preliminary page calculations in a number of ways. If you have double spaced typewritten pages, divide the number of pages by 1.6 if you are planning a 6 x 9 inch book. Consider that there are about 250 words on a typewritten page and an average of about 350 on the typeset pages of this book (allowing space for at least one heading). Most word processing programs will tell you precisely how many words your manuscript contains. From this total, you can reach a rough estimate of the number of printed pages in your book.

Even better, use your "save as" command to save your manuscript as a new, separate file. (Some programs have a "copy this file" command.) Set your type size and margins to approximate the book's inside layout without double spacings and have your computer do the work for you. You'll have to adjust for the *front matter* (title page, table of contents, foreword), inside chapter headings and the *end matter* (an index, addresses). In your new "save as" file, add enough blank pages before and after your body text to represent these and you'll end up close enough to obtain a preliminary printer's quotation. The size and length of your book can change later, but so will your final printing quotation.

Another decision to make is whether to publish in paperback or hardcover. I strongly recommend paperback editions for first time publishers unless you are producing a full colour photography or art book, a book intended primarily for corporate sales or a very short print run of a never-before-published local history (which will be reprinted as a paperback). Hardcovers cost more to produce resulting in high retail prices. Remember that you are not Margaret Atwood or Pierre Trudeau. Publishing in hardcover will only make your entry into the book business more difficult because, as an unknown and as yet unproven author, your first book will be too expensive for many shoppers. I know people who have taken the hardcover route with the intention of reprinting in paperback, but their hardcover print runs are still unsold several years later and they will never reprint. Trust me, stick to paperback editions until you really learn the ropes.

When Marion and I first decided to publish this book, we chose a size of 5.5 x 8.5 inches because it was cost efficient to print, convenient to read and easy for booksellers to stock on their shelves. This size fit well into smaller, less expensive mailing bags. We chose a paperback format to keep our costs down, to allow a reasonable retail price and to fit within our publishing budget. We decided the length of the book before we started writing. With the first printing, we felt that 128 pages would a) allow us to go into detail about the topic; b) fall within a general industry standard of actual thickness in relation to size and price; and c) just as importantly, conform to a standard book printer's layout to achieve maximum cost efficiency (*see Chapter 6*). This was a rough plan that changed somewhat as we worked.

To first estimate how long our proposed manuscript should be, Marion and I took the calculation I gave earlier and reversed it. A typeset book of 128 pages then becomes a word processed manuscript of about 160 pages. To allow for our preliminary pages, chapter breaks, section headings, a few illustrations and an index, we allocated 28 book pages. Our calculation was as follows:

Finished book, typeset, 5.5 x 8.5 inches:	128 pages
Reserved for preliminary pages, chapter breaks, illustrations:	- 28pages
Number of typeset pages:	100 pages
	100 pages x 1.6
Number of typed pages on 8.5 x 11 in. bond, double spaced:	160 pages

While adjustments and alterations can and should be made up to the final production stages, we were able to make other plans and projections because we started by defining the limits of the book.

SECURING A PRINTER'S QUOTE

Defining your format and page length early is absolutely necessary. You will need price estimates from printers in order to develop an idea of the costs involved in manufacturing your proposed book. Understanding and controlling your printing costs is one of the key factors in learning how to make money in the publishing business. It is important here to learn an acceptable way of breaking down the various physical aspects of the book into terms that a printer can evaluate and on which an accurate cost estimate can be provided.

Organizing the Details

As you develop your book plan, contact book printers and discuss printing details with them. Printers are in the business of helping you. They are accustomed to working with first time publishers and will do their best to answer all your questions. A printer can advise you on standard papers used in the book industry or suggest alternatives if you have special needs. You may need a particular type of coated paper (glossy or matte) if you have colour photographs or you may want the durability of heavier paper for a cookbook. Most book printers have sample kits or bound paper samples to help you decide on a paper stock.

Talk to printers about submitting your book on computer disk or laser printed printer-ready pages. Check to make sure your computer software and system are compatible with theirs. If you plan to have black and white illustrations or full colour photographs, discuss the best way of handling these. Black and white photos may need to be halftoned; colour photographs will need colour separations. It helps to be close to your printer so you can visit the office to view samples and be available for consultations before printing, but in these days of overnight couriers, fax and e-mail it is not absolutely necessary. Most large book printing companies have local sales representatives to work with customers unable to reach their head offices.

Presenting a Call for Quotations

The following is an example of how your information can be presented to receive as accurate a printing estimate as possible:

Call for Quotations

Name of book: A working title is quite all right.

Quantity: 1) 500 2) 1000 3)2000 4) 5000

Size: 5.5 x 8.5 in. (or 6 x 9 or 8.5 x 11 as standard sizes)

Number of Pages: 128

Inside Stock: 60 lb. matte offset (whichever paper is chosen).

Cover Stock: 10 pt. Cornwall with .5 mil plastic lamination, outside only. (Take a book you like to the printer and ask what weight of cover stock was used. Discuss plastic cover coatings.)

Inside Ink: Black throughout (or specify the number of colours you want). Black is considered one colour.

Cover Ink: 1. *Four colour process cover.* (You will supply a colour transparency and/or colour photo or your own colour separations with a colour proof if you've had them done locally.)

Cover Ink: 2. *Two colour cover.* (Two colour graphic art work can be effective as a cost cutting option.)

Preparation: *1a.* Inside text supplied on disk for output direct to negatives
1b. Inside artwork supplied as originals.
Printer to prepare and place where indicated.

(Note: Some printers do not want scanned graphic images on disk. It is felt that the quality of home scanning is not of sufficient quality to reproduce as well as it should.)

Preparation: 2. Camera ready. (This means your material is ready to go directly to the camera department for photographing and needs no additional work.)

Preparation: 3. Manuscript only: printer to prepare final layout. (You want to know the costs if the printer does all of the production work; or you may choose to do some, but not all of the preparation work yourself.)

Artwork: (a) 15 black and white photographs supplied. Printer to prepare, size and position.
(b) 6 line drawings supplied by publisher. Camera ready to size, no reductions (if the drawings fit the book page).

Binding: Perfect bound (or sewn, spiral, coil or as desired).

Bindery: Shrinkwrapped in bundles (or packed in pre-printed boxes. You can ask for separate quotes for each form of packaging).

Miscellaneous: Add any other needs you have.

F.O.B.: The address where the books will be shipped on completion. You pay the freight charges from the printing shop to this address. You can specify if you want the books to arrive Collect (you pay the freight on delivery) or ask to have the freight pre-paid and added on to your printing bill. The latter should be less expensive. You will not have to pay freight if you pick the books up yourself. If this is your intention, put the name of the printer after F.O.B.

Delivery Date: Specify when you want to receive the books. Allow three to six weeks for the printing.

Insert your own specifications and secure cost estimates from at least three different printers. Where you want the costs of options, number them as shówn in the example so the printer will know you want separate prices. Give each printer exactly the same specifications so you can compare costs. All quotations should be forwarded to you in writing. Note whether the quotes you receive are subject to change or additional charges and whether the prices are firm. Paper costs and labour charges change often so have your first quote re-confirmed within a month of sending your copy to the printer. Don't hesitate to have the printer confirm the price again after receiving your material just to be doubly sure there have been no changes or misunderstandings.

HOW PAYMENT IS MADE

Printers usually expect to be paid a third of the total bill on receipt of your material, one third when you receive your proofs and the balance when your books are printed. Most new publishers must pay the balance owing before the books are shipped; some printers will expect the balance when you receive your books or within 30 days. Printers will occasionally allow extended terms of payment, but may also charge premium interest rates.

TAKING DELIVERY OF YOUR BOOKS

It is hard to visualize the amount of space a press run of books will require. If you don't think you have adequate space in your home, you'll have to make storage arrangements. A warehouser or larger publishing firm may accept your print run for a minimal amount of warehousing rent. Your distributor might also have room for all your books for a fee. You can rent a public mini-warehouse cubicle for a low monthly cost. A warm, dry garage or basement of your own will eliminate storage costs.

Count your books when they arrive, multiplying the number of copies marked on each carton by the number of cartons. Count the number of books in at least two cartons first. Be aware that printers' contracts allow for a plus or minus 10% margin of the ordered amount as "proper delivery" on completion of your order. This guards the company against spoilage. If you receive more copies than ordered, you may or may not be charged for them depending on your agreement. Overages are usually invoiced at a nominal cost per book. If you receive 10% fewer copies, the printer is under no obligation to adjust your bill.

READ THE FINE PRINT

Most quotation sheets are printed on both sides. On the back you'll find a list of clauses, stipulations and exceptions that form the printer's standard business policy. Read it carefully and ask questions. As one example, it may be the printer's policy to claim ownership of all negatives and plates. This is a problem if you decide to re-print with another company. If there is any likelihood of this, have the clause deleted or changed in writing at the outset. Go over each point until you are satisfied with the agreement before you accept services.

CHOOSING A PRINTER

It is important to know that there are huge differences between a commercial printer and a book printer. A book printer is a company that specializes in printing books. The staff is experienced and knowledgeable about the requirements involved in producing a professional looking book. The shop is equipped with the technology necessary to manufacture quality books by the most cost efficient methods possible. Because book printers are focused on a specialized field of printing, they are more likely to offer you sound advice, more reliable service and, generally, better prices than printers who do not specialize in books.

A commercial printer, on the other hand, operates a shop where there is not necessarily a narrow focus of specialization. This kind of shop makes money on various printing jobs such as business cards, product labels and advertising brochures. No matter how good the quality of printing is for these items, commercial printers are seldom experienced in or aware of the details necessary to make your book look professionally produced by industry standards. These details can be critical to the success of your book.

Books produced by small commercial printers are often identified immediately by people in the book industry. The paper stock used for the cover or the interior pages may not be of a type commonly seen in trade books. There may be little consideration given to the aesthetic appeal of the interior layout. This can also apply to typestyles. Typestyles used on business cards have no place in the book industry.

To be fair, a commercial printer cannot take all the blame for a poorly produced or overpriced book. As the customer, you make the final decisions approving paper stocks, layout, type and costs. The printer may make suggestions which you will have to evaluate based on your research and budget.

More printing companies are developing their capabilities to produce short print run books in recent years. Occasionally, you *can* obtain a competitive price for a book project at a smaller company. Be business-like in your approach. Discuss the type of equipment and methods of production that will be used. What computer system is used and is this system compatible with yours? Can the shop handle plastic lamination? Perfect binding? Shrinkwrapping? How much of the work will be contracted out and will this cost extra? How much extra?

I believe that books with a projected press run of 2000 copies or more, with a market appeal beyond a very specific locale, should always be placed with a large professional book printer. I base my opinion on the now hundreds of poorly printed books that have come my way as a distributor and my past experiences in trying to sell these books to retailers. It is not my job to make excuses to a bookbuyer for a poorly manufactured book. There is no excuse that will bring forgiveness for a book that has been poorly bound and falls apart in the hands of a customer on first reading. In fact, the sales potential of these books is so dramatically impaired by poor appearance that even the most interesting, well written book will not be easily sold.

Keep in mind that the cheapest job is not always the best job. Ask the printer to refer you to other publishers who have used the company's services and then check with those publishers. Listen carefully to the recommendations or cautions of these former customers. If they were unhappy, chances are you will be too.

6
The Printing Process

LEARNING THE BASICS

Enormous changes have taken place in the printing industry since this book was first written. Even as this new edition comes off the press, there will have been more changes in production and printing technology. While you don't have to become a technological wizard, it *is* important that you understand at least the basics of the printing process. You control the publishing budget and will need to know how your book will be manufactured to make the best use of your money. An understanding of book printing and its special terms will help you to communicate better with a printer. It will also help you to reduce costs and increase your chances of making money by taking production methods into consideration prior to finalizing your material.

THE IN-HOUSE DESIGNER

If you wanted to do nothing more than provide a printer with a perfectly presented manuscript on disk, the printer would pass it on to a staff member who is skilled at book design. The designer would create a basic layout for your book on a computer. This would include choosing a book format, deciding how to lay out the interior text, where and how to place the graphics or illustrations and choosing typestyles, among many other details. The work done by the printer's designer is very much the same as work done by a highly regarded desktop publishing company. In other words, you are paying to have someone do all of the production work for you.

SUBMITTING PRINTER-READY MATERIAL

According to one book manufacturer in Winnipeg, there is currently a 50/50 split between material submitted on computer disk versus laser printed printer-ready pages. At the time of writing, less than 1% of their customers were still submitting pasted up copy. The prognosis for the future, however, is for an increase in the number of jobs submitted on computer disks. This increase is attributed to improvements in home computer programs, people's ability to master these programs and the printer's ability to adapt, convert and use the data submitted.

Laser Printed Pages

Printer-ready pages are your very final page copies. They have been triple checked, proofread and certified by you to be exactly as you intend with no mistakes. You've printed them on a good quality laser printer with a relatively new toner cartridge, using top quality paper. Text outputted from a laser printer is measured in dots per inch or *dpi*. Laser prints should be 600 dpi or higher to result in really sharp black type that will reproduce well at the printing house. Laser printed originals should be printed out all at once to avoid any fluctuations in toner density.

The cost of submitting laser printed pages to the printer versus submitting your book on a computer disk seems to vary from printer to printer. If you submit laser printed pages that originate from a publishing program, be sure to add *crop marks* to your final laser copies. The printer's camera department needs these as positioning marks when photographing your originals. These marks are also used to determine the trim size of your finished book.

Laser printed pages of straight text are considered to be "camera ready" by printers. This means that the pages will go directly to the camera department where they will be photographed. If you have illustrations to be placed into your book layout, some camera work may have to be done to prepare them for printing. You may be asked to supply the originals so that the printer can re-shoot them as halftones (black and white photographs) or create colour separations (colour photographs or colour illustrations) that can be added into the spaces you left for them in your book layout. Halftones and colour separations have to do with the way dots of black or colours reproduce when printed. For the best results, consult with your printer.

The highly specialized cameras used by book printers are enormous, using film that can accommodate 16 book pages of this size, being one half of a 32 page signature.The resulting large negatives are developed in much the same manner as your own photographs at a film processing lab.

Computer Disks

When you submit your book to a printer on disk, it essentially bypasses both the designer (you've done all that at your end) and the camera department. Where laser printed pages are photographed first by the camera department and then turned into negatives, books supplied on disk can be outputted directly to film. Instead of printing to paper as you might at home, the computer prints directly to a negative film. I am told that this process results in sharper images and crisper type than those resulting from photographing laser printed pages. Just appearing in the printing industry is a new machine that will eliminate even this step in the printing process. Instead of printing to a negative, it allows printers to output from a computer directly to the metal printing plate.

Using present technology, your disk is first loaded into the printer's computer and checked to see that the formatting is retained. Always send a hard copy printout of your pages with the computer disk as a check against the computer version. Your hard copy is a perfect mirror of your finished book pages. If you have illustrations, the printer can process and insert them in the correct format and size into their computer version of your book.

Once the formatting has been checked over and any graphics have been inserted, the computer technician then uses specialized software to place your pages on a grid that will result in a printing signature or *imposed film*. Just as the camera department fixes single pages onto one large grid that is photographed, so also does the computer technician, albeit on the small screen of a computer monitor. Once the signatures are laid out, the electronic command is given telling the computer to send your book to a machine called an *image setter*. In a matter of minutes, the final negatives print out.

FINAL PROOFING

The printer should send you a *blueline proof*. The blueline proof is created from your negatives and is a single entire copy of the book. This proofing stage represents your last chance for corrections and changes at this point will always involve additional expense. Proofing is especially difficult since you will feel that everything was perfect when you sent it to the printer—or so you thought. Proofread, or have someone else proofread your cover, front and back, as well as all of your titles, headings and subtitles. It is very easy to miss the most obvious. Check your proof for correct alignment of pages, making sure the borders are uniform throughout. Be sure the page numbers run sequentially and that they appear in the correct corners for odd and evenly numbered pages. Read the bottom four lines and the top four lines of each following page to make sure no lines or paragraphs have been missed due to hidden text in your publishing program. Are the captions under photographs correct? Are the photographs in the right places, and right side up? Double check your ISBN. Is it correct on the inside of the book as well as on the outside back cover? Colour photographic proofs or *colour keys* are more difficult for the novice to assess. You may wish to seek the advice of someone experienced in evaluating them. You will be asked to approve your proof in writing. Once you've given approval there is no turning back without accepting full responsibility for any oversights or mistakes in the final product.

MASKING

No matter which technical method is used to create the negatives, the large film signatures are then *masked*, or put into a type of flexible frame. This is done very carefully to ensure that the registration marks are true, particularly important where colour printing is involved. Graphic elements such as halftoned photographs will be stripped into the negative at this point. Holes are then punched at the edges to allow for positioning, both in the plate burner and ultimately on the press.

THE PLATING PROCESS

The masked negative is now paired with a blank printing plate and placed in a machine called a *plate burner*. Printing plates are usually metal, although paper plates are sometimes used for very tiny print runs. (Paper plates are designed for one time use. Don't let a printer talk you into using anything other than a metal plate. You will want to re-print your book eventually; there should be no need to pay for plates again.) Printing plates are made with a coating of a photosensitive material. Inside the plate burner, a very strong flash of light is allowed to strike the negative and pass through the images of type and illustrations. This light causes the coating on the plate to react with the result that the negative (or mirror) images are transformed into positive ones on the plate. After the correct exposure time, the plate is put through a plate processing machine from which it emerges ready for the printing press.

ECONOMIES OF SCALE: SAVING MONEY

The size of the negative and the corresponding plate is important to both the printer and to you. Your printer can advise you on how many pages they can or will place onto a single negative or plate. Be aware that some page counts are more economical depending on the outer dimensions of the book. A book that measures 5.5 x 8.5 is possibly the most economical of all the standard sizes. A book of this size, printed by an established book printer, will be printed as 32 page signatures. This means that four signatures will yield a book of 128 pages, while 5 signatures will result in 160 pages. Should your page count be 162 pages, you'll be charged the full cost of processing a negative, a plate, the press time and paper costs as if it had 32 pages anyway. At worst, try to keep your page counts in increments of 16. If you are producing an 8.5 x 11 book, then 16 page increments are ideal. If your book is a very small paperback measuring 4.25 x 7 inches, it may be printed in 48 page increments. It may mean reducing your manuscript or expanding your front matter or even adding to the body text, but try to plan a book that fits your printer's best economies of scale.

PRINTING

The plates have arrived at the press. The press operator attaches the plates to large drums on the press, loads your paper stock, prepares the inks and starts full production of the printed sheets. When a book printer prints a one colour text job such as the inside of this book, both sides of a single sheet will be printed at the same time. This is called *perfecting* and saves time. If the job requires more than one colour, the same sheets can be put through more than once. Your original quotation allows for the number of times the paper will go through the press. The cost will depend on the type of printer you choose, the press used and its capabilities to print from one to four or more colours at the same time. Before you decide to publish a book in multiple colours, discuss colour printing with your printer and find out the most cost efficient way to add colour into your book design.

ASSEMBLY

Once the book pages have been printed , they are called *press sheets*. The press sheets are then put through a machine that folds them into finished signatures. Hignell Printing of Winnipeg has two folding machines that run continuously. One folds the press sheets into 32 page signatures, the other into 16 page signatures. This is another reason to stay with 32 and 16 page increments. Stick with the standards to save money. After folding, the signatures are put through a collating machine to form *book blocks* and bound, often on the same machine. Some small printers may rely on human hands to collate pages after they are folded by machine. Collating by hand means workers walking around a table picking up the printed pages, time after time after time. The latter form of collating is labour intensive. Whether it affects the final cost of your book is something that can be discovered by comparing price quotes and the various methods of manufacturing used by different printers.

BINDING

Book binding can take various forms. The most common and desirable for trade paperbacks is *perfect binding*. The measured, flat spine of the cover is glued to the folded, collated signatures. *Notched* perfect binding is a process where the edges of the stacked signatures have been perforated or notched during folding to allow better penetration of the glue and to provide extra strength to the binding. Perfect binding is done by machine, sometimes as a combined step as mentioned above or on a single piece of equipment. *Saddle stitching* is another form of book binding that is used in trade paperbacks. Magazines are often saddle stitched or held together by staples in the centre gutter. It is less expensive for small books, but it has significant disadvantages. Saddle stitched books are disliked in the trade book market because they do not have a flat, printed spine to attract buyers when placed spine out (or *spined* in booksellers' terms) on a store shelf. Customers must make the effort to pull a book out to read the title. It becomes difficult for both the customer and the bookseller when visually searching a shelf. A saddle stitched book can lose sales by hiding between other books.

Other forms of binding are designed according to the end use of the book. *Coil, spiral, wiro* and *cerlox binding* are chosen for cookbooks and manuals to keep them fully open at specific pages for "hands off" use. Each form of binding has positive and negative aspects to consider. Coil, spiral and wiro bindings present the same problem as saddle stitched books with poor visibility when placed spine out on bookstore shelves. Fold-around covers are sometimes designed for these bindings to create a facsimile printed spine. An extension of the cover allows the title of the book to appear either inside or around the coil/spiral/wiro binding. Plastic cerlox binding can be printed with the title for shelf display, but it is relatively expensive. Some complain that the plastic cerlox will crack if not well packaged in shipping, while others say that under the same circumstances, the wiro binding can be crushed and bent.

There is now a new style of binding that strikes a compromise between the firmly glued or sewn spine of a trade paperback and the hands-off intentions of coil binding. This new "lay-flat" binding, known by the trademarked name *Otabind*, looks just like a perfect bound book. The folded pages are bound firmly to each other and not to the inside spine of the cover. The cover is glued at the edges of the spine. The flexibility of the spine coupled with the way the pages are bound allows the reader to flatten the book and have it stay flat while in use. Many publishers are choosing this form of binding for specific types of books such as cookbooks, guidebooks and manuals. I have not heard of any problem with this type of binding and it appears to be a good option.

Sewn and *case* binding are forms of binding that are used for hardcover books (although paperback books can also be sewn). Library or deluxe editions are bound with the idea of quality and durability in mind. For very thick books, these types of bindings are almost essential to accommodate the volume of pages. Dustjackets are printed separately and folded around most hardcover books. Your printer can provide you with detailed information on the various types of binding available.

PACKAGING

Book printers used to routinely shrinkwrap finished books, but few if any include it now without an additional charge. Shrinkwrapping is worth an extra expense if you can afford it. Unfortunately, it's also one of those costs that you may have to jettison at the last minute as a budget cut. Heat-sealed plastic wrap protects the books in shipping and helps reduce scuffing with handling. Often you can specify the number of books in a bundle. In most cases, however, the quantity per bundle will depend on the thickness of each book and how many will fit in the printer's cartons. If you have the choice of bundles containing 5 or 10 books, choose the higher number. You can increase your sales if you have a fast selling book by encouraging booksellers to order by the shrinkwrapped bundle rather than in odd or lower quantities.

Custom boxes are another form of packaging available at additional cost. While you can order boxes for single books as a convenience or marketing device (for specialty books likely to be purchased as souvenirs or overseas gifts requiring shipping by the consumer), they are an expensive luxury. Cookbooks are sometimes boxed in lots of 10 or 12 with the name of the cookbook custom printed on the outside of the box. The printed boxes serve as an advertisement. They are convenient, but the small boxes should be taken into consideration when shipping. Be careful of shipping methods where you may be charged by the piece or carton rather than by the total weight of the shipment. You can make money and save freight charges in some instances by firmly taping two or three boxes together or by packing a number of the smaller boxes into big cartons when shipping larger orders.

Book Design 7

BOOK DESIGNERS

Book designers are highly paid individuals who earn their money by creating book covers that will capture the eye of the purchaser and encourage sales. They also create interior layouts that are meant to be appealing, easy to read and cost effective. The designer uses the space available to incorporate the content in such a way as to get the maximum visual appeal for the least amount of expense. With their knowledge of the printing process, book designers can decide where best to place a series of colour photographs so that the publisher does not have to pay for any more colour work than necessary to achieve sales impact. Grouping colour photographs into signatures is an example of a cost saving method. It is less expensive than colour photographs placed randomly throughout a book and still very effective in terms of customer impact.

As consumers, we are often not conscious of the specific details of a designer's work. We are impressed by the cover of the book and influenced by the appearance of the inside layout without stopping to reason why. Good book design, like good editing, is a behind-the-scenes talent. The following will help if you plan to be involved in the design of your book.

TYPESTYLES

Even the most basic home computers now come with font packages built into basic software or word processing programs, giving us all a capability that was once the exclusive domain of the huge typographic machines owned by printers. Two broad categories of type are *serif* and *sans-serif*. Serif typestyles have "hooks" or serifs on each letter; the most easily recognized is the one used for Roman numerals. Sans-serif does not have "hooks" or "feet". This book type is serif. It's specific name is *Times New Roman*, a variation of the *Times Roman* font commonly used in book publishing. The names can vary depending on the company that produces the software. Most typestyles include a range of sizes with options for boldface type and italics to allow for special emphasis of titles or sub-headings.

Font is the name given to a type of a particular style and size. *Leading* describes the space between the lines of type. Type size is measured in *points*, the width of a line in *picas*. Once the typestyle is chosen, it's size is expressed in numerical values, such as 11/13 point. The font we use measures 11 points high with 13 points of leading or space between lines, expressed in printing vernacular as "11 on 13". The size of the type depends on how much copy you have, the line width selected and the number of printed pages you want. One word of caution: don't be tempted to go down to tiny type sizes just to fit in more words. People are very conscious of readability and tiny type can ruin sales.

PRELIMINARY PAGE LAYOUT

There is a standard layout procedure for the beginning of a book, also called the *front matter*. If you examine books produced by large publishing houses, you'll see a common pattern. A general guideline for a formal preliminary page layout is as follows:

Page 1: Half-title page. This is the very first page the reader sees and usually contains only the title of the book without the author's name. The title should be placed about a third of the way down from the top. (Mass market book publishers sometimes print review excerpts on this page to grab the reader's interest.)

Page 2: Blank. Nothing is printed on the back of the half title page. (The right hand page and the left hand page are referred to as *recto* and *verso* pages.) The blank verso page helps to draw the eye to the title page on the opposite right hand side.

Page 3: Title page. Now the full title of the book appears with the name of the author below, and close to, the title. The author's name shouldn't be much lower than about two thirds of the way down the page. Near the very bottom, the publisher's company name appears. Below the company name is often the name of the city where the publishing company is located.

Page 4: Copyright page. This follows on the back side of the title page and is usually designed with the copy flush left. At the top goes the author's name, the copyright symbol and the year of copyright. The publisher's declaration of publishing rights follows this. Beneath goes the CIP information and the ISBN number *(see Chapter 9)*. At the bottom is more information with the publisher's name and address. Occasionally, the name and address of a distributor is listed as well. The phrase "printed and bound in Canada" should appear at the bottom (unless printed elsewhere) and is important to include if you have any intention of selling your book in foreign countries. Some printers automatically print their names beneath this phrase. Although it is a form of advertising, it also shows that a printer has confidence in the quality of the work.

Page 5: Dedication page. This is your opportunity to honour some person(s), living or not. The dedication should appear about a third of the way down the page, though this is not a hard and fast rule. You may choose to include one or not.

Page 6: Blank

Page 7: Table of Contents.

Page 8: List of illustrations or blank. The table of contents, if necessary can run onto this page.

Page 9 & 10: Preface, or Acknowledgements. If the Preface (or Acknowledgement) doesn't require two pages, it can go on page 9, leaving page 10 blank.

Page 11 & 12: Introduction. Again, if the introduction is very short, only one page may be necessary. If this is the case, the introduction should go on page 11, leaving page 12 blank.

Page 13: Photograph, map or illustration on either page 13 or on 12. If on page 12 then copy begins on page 13.

If on page 13, then page 14 is blank and copy begins
on page 15.

Page 15: Copy begins here. Books always begin on the recto
or right hand page.

As you may notice, this type of beginning layout requires many pages and may not be best for your book. If you publish for the academic market, you may want to use it. I prefer a shortened layout to allow more pages for text. Here's a shortened layout:

Page 1: Title page
Page 2: Copyright page
Page 3: Table of Contents
Page 4: Acknowledgements or Preface or Special Note
Page 5: Blank or Dedication
Page 6: Blank or photograph or map
Page 7: Copy begins

Using the shortened version or adapting in relation to the more formal preliminary page layout is important if you need to adjust the overall layout later. These rules are not absolute and are only intended as general guidelines used by publishers. As you may notice, I switched front matter pages in this book. It seemed more natural to have the second edition Preface appear ahead of the three pages comprising our new Table of Contents.

BODY COPY LAYOUT

There is no rigid way of laying out the interior typeset copy of a book. You can learn different techniques by looking at books produced by professionals and observing how they have handled layout. Cookbooks have fairly standard layouts with colour photos sometimes acting as dividers between chapters. A guide book or a history book usually has definite chapter or section breaks. Will each new section begin on the right hand page, or is it appropriate for the chapters to run consecutively, sometimes beginning on the left, sometimes on the right? You decide this. The width of your margins is very important and worth a conversation with your printer. You must leave enough room around your type for binding and trimming to size.

White space is blank or unprinted space. It is important to the eye. If there is not enough white space in a book the type appears crowded and is difficult to read. Adequate white space allows the reader to relax with the words. Consider the impression that print and space create when deciding your font size and leading. Small, cramped copy is often the result of not working out the relationship between the length of the manuscript and the number of pages in the finished book. Use white space constructively to offset the copy or to enhance illustrations.

PAGE NUMBERING

Keep in mind that your page numbering system may differ from the physical count of first few pages of a book. Many publishers use lower case Roman numerals for the pages that make up the front matter. Looking at the shortened layout version of the front matter, the Roman numeral *iii* would appear at the bottom of your first page of the Table of Contents and continue in sequence to the end of the front matter. No page numbers should appear on either the Title page or the Copyright page. The first conventional page number would appear on page 7, the page on which the body of the book begins. While chapter breaks of blank pages are counted in the numbering process, numbers should not be placed on them. Resume placing your page numbers on the first page of the next chapter. There are variations in page numbering systems. Follow the method that works best for your book.

COVERS

Almost everyone judges a book by its cover. In this industry, it's quite common to hear people remark, "It's got such a great cover," with the same kind of approval one gives to a fine vintage of wine or a good brew of beer. On the other hand, one also overhears comments such as, "It's a great book; what a shame the cover is so bad," as if the book is doomed forever. If the cover prevents the book from selling, it probably is doomed to a future in a dark basement.

To get an idea of how effective covers can be in displaying and selling books, go back to the bookstore and this time, study cover designs. Which ones really stand out and almost beckon you to come over and touch them? Choose a few that are really exceptional and study the various elements that have been used to create the effect. Decide what it is that makes the cover so attractive.

Cover Coatings

Glossy book covers have a distinct appeal for certain types of books. Most books with glossy covers show better under bookstore lights and convey a distinct sense of "bright, shiny and new". Know what you want prior to printing as there are several ways of achieving a glossy cover.

Plastic lamination is a technical process where a very thin film of plastic is bonded to the printed covers with heat and pressure. There is a certain amount of skill required on the printer's part in relation to tension, temperature and the material used and not all printers are able to provide this service. The plastic lamination is applied only to the printed side of the cover and never to the inside. Any signs of peeling or covers that curl outward indicate a poor job. Plastic lamination is the most durable cover coating and is the most widely used process for creating glossy covers for trade books. Matte lamination is the result of the same process but instead provides a flat or non-glossy finish instead. Many literary book publishers have opted for matte lamination. You'll easily find examples of these types of lamination in any bookstore.

Press varnish and coated paper stock are two other methods often offered by commercial printers as a substitute for the plastic lamination. Press varnish is applied on a printing press as a liquid. Depending on the type of varnish, the liquid dries to a shiny or matte finish as pre-determined by you and the printer. Like plastic lamination, the varnish seals the inks used on the cover to inhibit scuffing. The main drawback with press varnish on perfect bound books is its tendency to crack when a book is opened and it is not as scuff-resistant as plastic lamination. Some paper stock is pre-coated in the manufacturing process and has a somewhat glossy appearance even before printing. If you select coated stock for your book cover, remember that the inks are put on top of the glossy paper surface. Without a coating over the inks, you will not have the added protection against scuffing. This merits much consideration since books are handled and moved in bookstores and will scuff easily with nothing to blame but the coating itself. Inks printed on coated stock also are not as easily absorbed by the paper and may take some time to dry. Of all the options, the plastic lamination process used by book printers is preferable.

Colours

Colours used for book covers often go through a long process of selection in a combined effort between the book designer and the publisher to choose the most appropriate and effective colour schemes possible. Selecting a colour scheme for a book cover can be a difficult decision. Sometimes the content of the book is a factor in selecting cover colour. A local history book might suggest sepia tones and light browns for cover colours. Many business book covers are combinations of bold blues, reds and yellows. There is, of course, an entire field of psychology related to colour response. Some colours are deemed more attractive to people than others and are thought to influence buying decisions. Rich blues, bright reds and white have been popular cover colours, though recent times have seen a design trend away from really bold, strong colours and some movement towards the use of muted and pastel colour combinations. Glossy black covers have also proven to be very marketable for higher priced editions and are said to convey an impression of quality. Be warned that black covers show finger-prints and mark very easily. Try to use colours effectively: if you plan to use a colour photograph on your cover, harmonize the border around it just as you would if framing a painting. Otherwise, spend your colour research time in the bookstore and work with a designer who is experienced in the creation of book covers.

Cover Design

While colour is certainly one aspect of cover design, there is also a great deal of planning that goes into the way the title is presented along with the graphic elements that illustrate the cover. The various components of the cover should be laid out to form a balanced, harmonious, holistic effect. If you've studied art, so much the better in understanding that the eye is captured by one aspect of a picture and then led to other parts of the picture before coming back to rest on the initial starting point. If we relate this to a book cover, our eye may be captured initially by the title, then drawn to look at the picture on the cover, the author's name, then back to the picture and brought to rest on the title again. All book covers are not designed this way, but it is one approach used quite consciously by publishers and designers.

Mass market paperbacks are excellent examples of covers that are designed for maximum eye appeal. Today's mass market covers are sometimes quite "glitzy" with strong use of colours, foil papers or metallic inks that aggressively seek to grab your attention in the bookstore. Linear designs with horizontal or vertical banners are often used and created with large store displays in mind. If you look at the way these books are displayed in chainstores, where rows and rows of the same book are placed facing outwards, you'll see what I mean. The same cover is sometimes printed in different colours, with the store receiving twenty copies that are blue and silver and another twenty copies that are red and gold. When these books are displayed together, the covers can form one huge design based on the repetitive design of each individual book. As a marketing technique, it is brilliant in every way. The use of foil on trade books is less common; foil covers are expensive and seldom seen on trade paperback books.

Back Covers

The importance of the back cover is often overlooked by first time publishers. The back cover is a perfect, permanent stand-in salesperson. Once the cover has attracted a potential buyer and inspired that person to pick up your book, you have a captive audience for a written sales pitch. That's the role that your back cover copy plays. The copy gives a synopsis of the book at a glance and contains enough well placed words to convince a reader that this is a "must-have" book. At the very least, the back cover copy should inspire the reader to open the book and look inside. The combined effect of the cover, the back cover and the interior layout, notwithstanding the price, should create a strong impetus for purchasing. Even if the topic is not one that particularly interests the person holding the book, if everything about the book is saying "Buy me! Buy me!" that person may think of someone else who would appreciate it and purchase it as a gift. Writing back cover copy is an art in itself—don't hesitate to hire someone to write it.

Back Cover Details: Barcodes, Subject Category, ISBN

It is now absolutely essential to have a barcode printed on the back cover of your book. Most of the largest stores will not consider buying a book that doesn't have one. Think of a grocery store. Cashiers no longer punch endless numbers into a cash register, they simply run the barcode of the item across a window that contains a small beam of light. This beam of light transmits the information on the barcode to the grocery store computer. This same sort of technology is well underway in the book industry. It's called *Point of Sale* or "P.O.S." Grocery barcodes contain information that is different from the information in the barcodes used by retail bookstores. The one on your book should be coded with the ISBN only. Hand scanners are used by many booksellers to transmit the ISBN in your barcode to their computer systems. This is faster and more efficient than typing the 10-digit number on a computer keyboard. Bookstore computers may also have inventory management programs such as *BookManager*. In the event of a sale, the computer records that a copy has sold and reduces the computer inventory. This kind of computerization allows the bookseller to assess sales and inventory and to reorder quickly and easily.

Barcodes can be obtained from numerous sources. Most book printers can create a barcode for your book. There are companies that specialize in them. (Check your local telephone book.) Be clear that you want the *Bookland EAN* (European Article Numbering) code which is the code on which the book industry works. Ask the company if they guarantee the accuracy of their barcodes. All reputable companies will. If disaster strikes, and you discover your barcode is wrong after your book is printed, barcode stickers can be made up to place over the original ones. The stickers work well for books currently in print that require a barcode. Be aware that a distributor will charge for adding stickers to your books. Reputable bar code suppliers will provide the corrected stickers and reasonable added costs as a part of their guarantee, providing the fault is theirs and has not occurred in the printing process.

There are other bits of information to be accommodated in your back cover design. Stores now want the subject category and the ISBN printed on books. The ISBN is usually printed in numbers you can read at the top of the barcode. The barcode goes in the bottom right hand corner. If you want to be kind to booksellers' eyes, include the ISBN in 14 point type in the lower left corner. The subject category can go at the top left and can include up to three categories. For example, if you've written a book on *How to Overcome Female Dependency*, your subject categories will be psychology, self-help and gender studies. While most booksellers will place your book in only one category, they will sometimes place it in two at the most. The subject category allows them to categorize it in the computer without having to guess. The real purpose of adding all this information is to accommodate the retail market. Stores need this detailed information easily available when handling books and working with computers.

Many stores now want the price to be printed on the book. I hesitate to add this since many first time publishers are forced to change their prices after printing due to inaccurate costing or unforeseen circumstances. If you have taken *all* of the factors of production, printing, distribution, relative pricing and promotion into consideration and are truly sure of your retail price, print it on the book. If not, buy or borrow a price stickering device and use price stickers after publishing.

Printing the Spine

Not all books can be placed with the front cover facing out on a bookshelf. New books receiving major publicity are usually displayed facing outward by booksellers. Almost all trade books are "spined" or placed spine out on the shelves sooner or later. This is not something to be upset about, but more a case of space restrictions and practicality from the bookseller's point of view. I once had a letter from someone asking me to take over the distribution of a book. In the letter was a list of accounts to whom this person was no longer selling because the retailers were not displaying the book "properly." I don't think this publisher quite understood the economics of bookselling.

Printing the title of the book in clear type along the spine is necessary to assist in locating the book after it has been spined. The flat spines of perfect bound books accomodate type nicely. As a point of interest, booksellers asked us not to change the colour of the spine of this new edition because they have become used to searching for a red spine. If you are publishing a saddle stitched or staple bound book, you can help make your book more noticeable by printing the title, the author's name and the ISBN about 1/4 of an inch from the spine, running vertically down the back cover. You may be able to incorporate this into your front cover design as well. The book title will be spotted more easily from one side at least, and needs only to stick out a bit from the other books to catch an eye.

A Final Note About Covers

When the first edition of this book arrived from the printer, I was sick to discover that our printing instructions had not been followed. The blue ink that coloured the lettering was to have been screened to produce a pale, ice blue. Instead, the blue was printed in the same intensity as the strong red we had chosen for that edition and was not at all the effect we had intended. We learned to live with it and the print run sold anyway. Another publisher I know forgot to proofread her cover. She had been given permission to use a quotation given by a famous person. Imagine her embarrassment when the finished books arrived with a spelling mistake in the quotation. Fortunately, the mistake is not that obvious at a casual glance. This book is in stores and selling now, with profuse apologies made to the famous person. Mistakes like these do happen and few books are completely flawless. The point is to reduce the chances of mistakes on your book cover.

Covers are so important in the success of a first book that I cannot recommend strongly enough that you seek the services of a professional to do the cover design and production. Unless you are a graphic artist and can create truly professional looking cover illustrations, you'll need a good artist for the artwork. If you plan to have a colour photograph for the cover, make sure the original is of extremely good quality, be sure to have permission to use it and consult your printer. Research colour separations. Find someone who is experienced at reading colour proofs supplied by printers. A good design person will help you do all of this from choosing colours and typestyles to producing a cover design that will give you an edge in the marketplace. Any extra money spent on your cover in hiring the services of a professional will be well worth it.

PART SIX:
Marketing and Book Publishing

Nancy Wise

An example of a simple promotional sheet

Marketing 8

IDENTIFYING MARKETS

Different types of books and various markets are identified within the book industry. Books are categorized according to topic, the age group for whom they are written or by genre. Fiction, non-fiction and poetry are three genres. These can be further divided into adult, juvenile or children's books. Non-fiction can be divided into a variety of sub-categories from biographies, histories or self-help books to guide books, cookbooks, reference books or any of numerous special interest categories. You must know how to identify your book in relation to sales markets. Booksellers will want to place it in the correct subject category on their shelves. Those with computers will not have to guess when filling in the subject field of their computerized receiving systems.

Sales markets can be divided into at least four general segments. They are:

Trade. Trade sales involve books that sell in traditional outlets such as bookstores. The market focus tends to be on the general public. Books carried by bookstores are also identified according to format, size or price. *Mass market* books are "pocket size" with paper covers and are generally printed on low cost newsprint. These books are produced in very high quantity press runs and sold at low retail prices. Mass market editions rarely have colour pictures. While they are sold in bookstores, mass market books are also distributed by wholesalers to grocery stores, drug stores or any place where the wholesaler has a rack jobbing agreement. *Trade editions* by comparison are usually larger in size, available as paperback or hardcover and printed in smaller press run quantities with higher quality papers. Retail prices for trade book editions can range from about $6 to $75 and upwards. Mass market books seldom exceed $10 in price. Trade books are primarily intended for bookstore sales and tend not to be as widely available in other types of stores.

Educational. Books published for the educational market involve textbooks, reference books or any book of particular use in private or public school curriculum. There are publishers who specialize in producing books for the educational market. Sometimes a publisher who produces books for the trade market will have a book that will succeed in both the trade market and the educational market. Discounts in the educational market vary widely. Some publishers do not discount books published for this market or allow only very small ones. Smaller trade book publishers may offer up to 20% discount to schools and libraries, although some publishers offer 40% if the order meets an established minimum in either dollar value or the number of copies ordered. There are educational representatives and suppliers who sell primarily to schools; many bookstores also sell to schools. While school sales were once considered to be very lucrative, the nation-wide funding cuts of recent years have had a drastic effect on the educational market.

Libraries. Libraries used to represent a huge market in Canada for self publishers in the days when they purchased an enormous variety of books from many sources. Library budgets have also been severely reduced. Consolidated buying means obtaining as many books as possible through one ordering source. Ordering through specialized library wholesalers has become a more cost efficient means of buying for many libraries. While they do purchase trade paperbacks, many libraries prefer hardcover or board editions to withstand handling over time. Libraries that order from very tiny publishers do not expect, but certainly appreciate, a discount of any kind.

Non-traditional. Marion discussed the potential of these markets in her section on writing. To recap, non-traditional markets include sales made to special interest groups. Also considered to be aspects of the non-traditional market are corporate or premium sales. Selling your book in bulk quantities to a hotel sales manager for use as client appreciation gifts is an example of a premium sale since you are selling directly to a non-retail account. David Chilton's book, *The Wealthy Barber,* has also been extremely successful in the corporate market. I know of at least one national banking institution that used prominent counter displays to offer his book for sale to their customers. Corporate sales can be very profitable as can sales to special interest groups. Sales to non-traditional markets are especially attractive since the books are not subject to the returnability policy demanded by bookstores.

Identifying your book in relation to the established framework of the book industry will help you focus your sales efforts. There are many opportunities for selling your book. Each market is complex and requires research from a sales oriented viewpoint in order to develop an effective marketing strategy. Many books will cross over from one market to another. This book deals primarily with information that relates to publishing trade editions that will sell in Canadian bookstores.

MARKETING FACTORS

The term *marketing* is often used as a synonym for selling. While the end objective is to achieve sales, the term actually encompasses a broad range of factors that must be considered when any new product is introduced into the marketplace. Each new book is unique and can require individualized marketing strategies. It is the publisher that must develop these strategies in a process that involves research, contemplation, an awareness of opportunity and simply dogged work. Four marketing factors are directly related to publishing: (a) the product; (b) the price; (c) promotion; and (d) distribution. These factors are inter-related and influence one another. They are also subject to influence by a host of variables such as competition, book buying trends or the general economy.

THE PRODUCT

Your finished book will be the end result of decisions that you made about its content, format, cover design and all of the other production details discussed earlier. You will have researched the need for your book idea and checked out any possible competition in the same area of interest. What you have done is similar on a small scale to the product research that huge manufacturers undertake prior to the mass production of a new product. By speaking to bookstore owners and scores of friends and acquaintances, you are doing a consumer response test of your book idea.

Your book title is every bit as important as the physical appearance of your new book. Try to avoid very long cumbersome titles. Choose one that has meaning in relationship to the content of the book. Subtitles are also extremely important and effective because they add meaning to the title, or broaden the scope of the book's content by quickly communicating extra information or context. Subtitles sell books and are often under-used. Remember, too, that your book title may appear on a supplier's order form. A book titled, *The Gilly* may have no meaning to a bookseller until that person reads the subtitle: *A Flyfisher's Guide.*

Some booksellers will not buy the promise of a book. They need to see the finished product. Booksellers can seem highly enthusiastic about your ideas, yet delay ordering in quantity until they see the book for themselves. Don't be discouraged if a bookseller places only a small advance order. It simply means that the buyer wants to see what kind of job you've done with the physical appearance of your book. Your title, format, cover design, layout and price must pass muster. This is also true when looking for a distributor. Few, if any, will offer a sales agreement until the finished book is in their hands.

PRICING STRATEGY

A pricing strategy is essentially the process of determining your retail price in relation to your costs, the size and perceived value of your book and positioning the price in relation to other similar books already available. You have to ask yourself: how good is my book in comparison to other similar ones? What retail price will it bear and still make a profit? Working out a pricing strategy is more complicated that it was ten years ago. Several changes have taken place that warrant consideration.

In 1990, the federal government brought in the Goods and Services Tax or GST. Until then, books had been protected from taxation as cultural commodities. Despite persistent lobbying by representatives of the book community, GST was imposed on the sale of books at all levels of the industry. (It is only recently that GST has been eliminated from school and library purchases through a special rebate program.) Printers, publishers, authors, libraries, schools, wholesalers, distributors and book retailers became tax collectors overnight. Ultimately, it is the book buying public who bears the burden of paying extra for the freedom to read. Not long after the GST arrived, the book industry suffered another blow with the first of many increases in paper prices. The cost of printing books in Canada has risen, serving to drive book prices upward.

At one time, it was generally believed that shoppers were not as price conscious about books as they were about other consumer products. People were more apt to pay the publisher's list prices without question. Offering a discount to customers was a practice seldom used by bookstore owners. Changes in the book retail structure in combination with downturns in the general economy have led to a very different attitude today. The appearance of mega-bookstores as well as consumer wholesale outlets has led to entirely new marketing strategies which include a strong reliance on discounting as a means of attracting customers. The success of these stores has shown that the book-buying public is now very price conscious. The combination of all of these factors places publishers in a precarious position. Your pricing strategy must incorporate a retail price low enough to be attractive to book buyers, yet high enough to allow room for additional discounts in the event of competitive pressure.

You, the publisher, set a book's "suggested list price," suggested because ultimately you cannot stop retailers from selling the book for more or less than you suggest. Given that there are many factors to consider, one of the formulas for setting a retail price is to add up your production costs and then multiply by four or five. Whether you multiply by four or five depends on how competitive the price is with other books of a similar size already on the market. Soft cover guide books and cookbooks, for example, are presently priced in the $14.95 to $16.95 range. If your costs are such that your paperback guide book or local cookbook must sell for $24.95, then you may run into consumer price resistance.

ESTABLISHING A RETAIL PRICE
The retail price of your book should be worked out early in the planning stages of your project. Printing costs, desktop publishing costs, fees for an editor, illustrator or photographer and any additional production costs must be added together. An extra amount for interest on borrowed money and some consideration for your own time should also be determined. How much monetary value you place on your time is largely up to you. However, charging your time out at $30.00 per hour will have a drastic effect on the overall profitability of the book. It is more realistic to consider your time as an investment that will pay off over the long term, rather than as an immediate payback on your first print run. The idea is to produce a book and build a market that will continue to grow or at least remain stable over a period of years. As your book goes into second and third print runs, your production costs will drop. Your labour will pay off in higher profits over time.

Press Runs: *Large or Small?*
The size of your press run (how many books you print) will have a direct effect on your calculation of a retail price. The smaller your print run, the higher the cost per book. The price for printing 5,000 copies is always more cost effective than the printing price for 1,000 copies based on a per unit cost. The printer will charge a base amount just for initial set up costs in making negatives, plates and preparing the press for running your job. These costs can apply whether you have one book or one thousand books printed. After a certain point, the costs of additional copies basically become a matter of press time, paper stock and bindery work. Some printers will quote a dollar figure based on the first 1,000 copies printed with each additional thousand printed in the same press run charged at a smaller rate per copy. This means that you might have 5,000 copies printed for about twice what you'd pay for 1,000 copies. In the case of one quote I obtained for a small book, the cost for 1,000 copies was $2235. For 5,000 copies of the same book, the price was

$4640. By dividing the number of copies into each quotation, I arrived at a per book printing cost of $2.24 for 1,000 copies and a significant drop to $.99 per book on a 5,000 copy press run.

Deciding how many copies to print is difficult. If you work just the printing costs out on paper, it will be very tempting to opt for a large press run because of the economies in scale and the deceptively low cost per book. You must seriously consider how long it will take to sell 5,000 books. Consider, too, that a national bestseller in Canada is a book that sells 5,000 copies in its first year of release. If you are publishing a book of poems, it could take you as long as ten years to sell even a very small press run. If it is a regional guide book, they could sell within the first two or three years or sooner with good planning and hard work. In the latter case, you may want to decide whether your money will earn a better rate of investment if half of it is left in the bank collecting interest, or if all of it is tied up in books. I know self publishers who have chosen to test the market for their book with a first print run of just 500 copies. The objective was to test the demand, even at a substantial cost. As a rule, one should never print more copies than can be sold in one calendar year. Printing a moderate sized press run of 1,500-2,000 copies is an alternative. Your profit may not be as great, but neither will your risk.

Promotion Costs

Promotion costs must eventually be included in your cost calculations, but leave them out until you test the retail price you determine based on your production costs. Promotion costs include the value of sample copies given to reviewers and bookbuyers to gain sales. Work out a rough estimate of how many you plan to give away and remember that their value at cost will affect your overall profit margin. Mailing costs, phone calls and travel expenses to and from media interviews are all considered promotion costs. (The clothes you wear to the interviews are not.) Expect to spend money to promote your book. Allow approximately 5% of your retail price multiplied by the number of books printed. This will vary according to the nature of the book and its market and how hard you are willing to work to promote it. Since promotion costs are variable expenses (you will ultimately control how much you spend later), it is not common to include them in your production costs.

Total Your Production Costs

To determine an approximate retail price, first add your printing and production costs. The sum of these costs is divided by the number of copies you will print. It is this figure that is commonly multiplied by four or five. Do various calculations by adjusting the number of books you want to print. Look at the relationship between your costs and the size of possible print runs. Now take your test retail price and apply the discounts described below. Examine your profit margin. Be realistic and re-check your numbers several times. Once you are committed to a book project, mistakes become uncomfortable, if not disastrous.

Discounts to Consider

Retail and distribution discounts can come as a shock to the first time publisher. *(See Chapter 10)* The minimum standard trade discount expected by bookstores is 40% off the retail price. This seemingly huge amount is earned by the bookstore owner and goes towards paying overhead, including rent, utilities and staff, with a profit to support the business. Without bookstores, the public would have much more difficulty locating your books. If you handle your own sales without a distributor, your income from a book retailing at $14.95 less a 40% discount is $8.97 per book. Trade book distributors charge from 55% to 65% of the retail price for the services they provide. If you are printing a large press run, allow for this discount in advance. You will probably need a distributor to get your books into a wider sales network. Deducting an average of 60% from a retail price of $14.95, your income from a distributor is $5.98 per book. This discount includes the 40% minimum discount that the distributor must give the bookstores.

If you work these calculations out on a book financed with your own money, you might be discouraged to learn how little profit there is in self publishing. You may discover that there is no room to allow for a distributor or an independent sales rep. Printing small runs of 1,000 copies or less can mean doing all of your own sales and order fulfilment, so be prepared. But take heart, because the 40% discount need not apply to all of the books you sell. You can work out how many copies you will sell at full retail to friends and through direct mail orders and how many you will sell in bookstores. Let's say you estimate that 60% of 1,000 copies retailing at $14.95 will sell in your local bookstores and that 40% will sell at full retail if you undertake a direct mail strategy. This means that 600 copies will generate $5382 and the remaining copies will generate $5980. The total cash generated will be $11,362 or $2,392 more than selling them all in bookstores. This example is by no means hard and fast. It is one way of working out how much you could earn from a press run, recognizing that you will sell your books to different market segments.

Experienced publishers may ask whether the amount of time you spend producing, promoting and selling your book is worth it in financial terms. It is a question you must ask yourself: are you prepared to do the work and minimize the cost of your own time to learn the business? My belief is that very few self publishers earn substantial profits on their first books. With experience, one becomes much more pragmatic and business-like in dealing with second print runs or second books. Marion calls her first book an "expensive education."

Testing Your Price

If your production costs are $3.25 per book on a print run of 2,000 and you multiply your costs by four, your approximate retail price will be $13.00. Multiply by five and your retail price becomes $16.25. These are considered irregular prices in the book industry. Always work on standard prices based on one dollar increments, rounded to $.95. The $16.25 price will become either $15.95 or $16.95. But you decide that the book will perform better if the price can be kept under $15.00. Let's test a price of $14.95 and look at your minimum profit margin:

Proposed retail price:	$14.95
Less 60% distribution discount:	—$ 8.97
Subtotal:	$ 5.98
Less cost per book:	—$ 3.25
Gross profit/book:	$ 2.73

Minimum profit/book is $2.73 or approximately 18%

This means that even if *all* your books sold through a trade book distributor, you would receive an 18% gross profit on your cash investment. The more sales you make at full retail through direct mail sales or by selling to non-traditional markets, the higher your gross profit will be. Most publishers do make sales in other markets, without conflicting with the retail bookstore market.

Break-even Points

The critical factor and inherent risk in self publishing is the length of time it will take to sell enough books to cover your initial investment. When you reach the goal of selling enough copies of your book to recover your initial cash outlay, you will have reached what is called the *break-even point*. To calculate how many books you need to sell to reach this point, divide your costs of publishing by your average wholesale price. The following calculations are based on a retail discount of 40% in the first case and a distribution discount of 60% in the second.

1. a) Publishing costs x press run = initial investment
$3.25 x 2000 = $6,500.00

   b) Net income per book sold to retail outlets:
$14.95 - $5.98 (40%) = $8.97

So, (a) divided by (b) = break-even point

$6,500 divided by $8.97 = 724.63 or 725 copies

2. a) Publishing costs = $6500.00 (as before)

   b) Net income per book sold to a distributor:
$14.95 - $8.97 (60%) = $5.98

So, (a) divided by (b) = break-even point

$6500 divided by $5.98 = 1086.95 or 1087 copies

These calculations show that (1) if you sold all of your books at a 40% bookstore discount, you'd have to sell 725 copies to reach your break-even point; or (2) if you sold them all through a distributor at the larger discount, you would break even after selling 1,087 copies. Selling all of your books at the same discount is unlikely, so you will have to work out an average discount for your calculation. Estimate the number of copies you plan to give away and adjust for your promotional costs. Subtract this number from the total press run and base your calculations on the balance.

Publishing is a business venture, no matter how large or small the scale. One of the aims of business is to make a profit. Few people make enough to earn a full time living with a first book, but it can be profitable if you are objective with your calculations. How profitable depends in part on your skills as a business manager.

Relative Value

Multiplying costs by five will create a higher profit margin, but only if the book will sell at that price. If consumers feel your book is too expensive, or more than they are willing to pay, your sales will suffer. If the price is perfectly in line with others in the same genre, then your book is more likely to sell well or at least compete fairly within its market. You must choose whether to sell a few books slowly and recover a slightly higher profit per book, or to turn the book over faster at a lower price and get your money back in the bank as quickly as possible.

CHANGING YOUR RETAIL PRICE

Many self publishers discover the concepts of retail and distribution discounts after they have begun selling their books at a certain price. Some totally reject the discount system without really understanding it. One person I met had already decided never to sell his book to a bookstore rather than give up 40% of his money. Instead of changing the price of the book to allow for standard discounts, his idea was to travel across the country and sell a book to every discriminating person he met. The larger distribution discount was greeted with particular disdain: "No way! I'd rather build a bonfire under them and burn the lot."

Another response to book discounts is an attempt to get the

bookseller or the distributor to accept a lower discount. This is poor practice. It is asking someone else to subsidize your book and pay for your mistakes. You were supposed to have researched the industry and calculated a fair price.

A more business-like approach to discovering that you have underpriced your book is to change the price on your unsold stock. Stock that has been sold should remain at the original offered price and it will be up to you to keep track of those sales in the event they are returned. Whether you are increasing or decreasing the price, you should send out notices to retailers so they know that their next orders will arrive at a new price. If you are increasing the price, include some explanation. You can admit you made a mistake in calculating your costs. No one expects you to sell your book for less than you paid to produce it.

Decreasing the price is more complicated, depending on whether your books are out on consignment or have been invoiced on net 30 day terms. If your books are on consignment, find out how many are unsold and re-write your consignment invoice to reflect the new price effective on that date. For stores that have purchased your books on net 30 day terms, you can offer to credit stores with the difference between the old and the new price on the unsold copies. The credit should be formally written up and applied against future orders. If your book has been widely distributed and out on the market for some time, you could send out notices to all of the accounts stating that the new price will come into effect on a specific date.

Most of the booksellers to whom you have sold will have taken your books as returnable merchandise. Almost all books are purchased with this option as a standard business policy. At worst, the bookseller may opt to return all of the higher priced books to you for credit or refund. In most cases, they will accept a credit for the difference to save shipping and handling costs. Changing a price afterwards is awkward, but not impossible. It is awkward for the bookseller who is suddenly found with stock at two different prices and who may have to explain the difference to a customer. It also means extra paperwork for everyone. Changing your price is an option to be carefully considered but one that may lead to much more reasonable expectations in the long run.

Promotion 9

It has been said that a bestseller is made not by the quality of the author's writing, but by the amount and kind of promotion that the book receives. Promotion is the process of informing both the general public and the industry buyers that a book is special or worth buying. It is absolutely essential to develop a demand for your book and should continue over time in various forms as an on-going stimulus to sales. Book promotion has three general phases: 1) announcing the forthcoming publication; 2) informing prospective buyers (both retailers and the general public) about the content of the book; and 3) reinforcing previous information to sustain sales and widen your sales network. These three general phases can consist of both personal and non-personal promotion ranging from public readings to space ads and reviews in specialty publications or newspapers. Most publishers use a combination of each to communicate their message to potential buyers.

PRE-PUBLICATION PROMOTION

Pre-publication or advance promotion is important as the initial step in making others aware that you are about to publish a book. There are two things you need to begin the process. You must obtain an *International Standard Book Number* or ISBN. After receiving an ISBN, you must then apply for Canadian *Cataloguing in Publication Data* or CIP. Having this information will ensure that your book receives attention in those journals, magazines and catalogues that regularly include news of forthcoming books. As a third, but no less important step, be sure to have your book listed with the R.R. Bowker *Books in Print Plus Canadian* database by filling out their *Advance Book Information* or ABI forms.

PROMOTIONAL BENEFITS OF ISBN AND CIP

An ISBN is a ten digit number that is unique to your book. Books that are published without an ISBN are, in a sense, invisible in the general book system. The National Library in Ottawa is in charge of assigning these numbers, but has no way of knowing about your book if it is not registered with them. The onus is on publishers to contact the ISBN office. *(see Addresses)* In our age of computers, a book without an ISBN is like an individual without a Social Insurance Number and is excluded from most of the benefits afforded otherwise.

Almost all booksellers rely on the ISBN for identifying and ordering books. There may be several books on the market with exactly the same title; the ISBN is the unique numerical code that identifies one book as being distinct from another. The national chainstore Chapters Inc. will not order a book without an ISBN since all ordering and inventory is computerized at their head office in Ontario. Once your book has been authorized for purchase by the Chapters head office, you can promote your book to the manager of your local chain store outlet. If the manager can call up your ISBN on the store's computer system, it provides verification and may lead to an order. Some privately owned bookstores will make up a temporary ten character code to allow entry of a title into their computer systems; be sure they will want to change it when you can supply them with an ISBN.

When Marion and I decided to re-write this book, we had to assign a new ISBN to distinguish it from the first edition. Although it has the same title, the content has been substantially changed, making it a very different book. Had we simply reprinted the first edition with very minor changes to the text, it would still be considered essentially the same book and no change of an ISBN would have been necessary. We also had to apply for new CIP due to the change in the ISBN.

Cataloguing in Publication Data is extremely important as free advance publicity since books with CIP are automatically listed in several trade publications that are circulated to bookstores and libraries across Canada. Obtaining an ISBN and CIP will trigger certain agencies to send you forms for free listings in publications such as *Canadian Books in Print* and *Quill & Quire's* "Forthcoming Books." These listings provide buyers with the information they need to order and these orders will generally come direct to you as the publisher. The latter is a benefit of the ISBN which is linked to the address you supplied when first applying.

Cataloguing in Publication Data can be obtained by calling the National Library or one of their many regional offices. This information can be found at the back of this book under our CIP and ISBN quick list. There are forms that must be completed and returned to the originating CIP office. You must have your ISBN before you can make this application. Within a week or two you'll receive a small slip of paper which at first glance appears to be inconsequential. This information, however, is of vital importance to library sales and must be reproduced exactly as supplied to appear on the copyright page of your book. Each number and letter provided by the CIP office means something within the library cataloguing system, so be sure to proofread carefully. By printing the CIP in your book, you will save individual libraries the expense of cataloguing your title. It costs a library around twenty dollars to manually catalogue a book and this expense can act as an inhibitor to purchasing if the library is operating within a strict budget.

CANADIAN TELEBOOK AGENCY

The Canadian Telebook Agency (CTA) is responsible for a national electronic ordering system developed to increase the efficiency of the book distribution system in Canada. It administers an industry-funded communications network that links member bookstores, libraries and wholesalers with their suppliers. This system allows a bookstore, for example, to electronically transmit many orders to a range of suppliers also linked to the system by the specialized CTA software and computer modems. The supplier receives the order electronically; the bookstore's order can then be printed out as a hard copy for invoicing, packing and shipping. Newer developments allow the supplier to not only acknowledge the receipt of the order in the office, but also to electronically acknowledge, order line by order line, which books are in stock and available for shipping immediately. Large companies are able to integrate the Telebook order directly with their invoicing software programs thus avoiding the need to re-enter the original order.

The Canadian Telebook Agency used to administer a database of Canadian book titles and ordering sources. In recent times, the further development and administration of this Canadian database has been turned over to an American company that specializes in maintaining and producing bibliographic databases. R.R. Bowker Data Collection Centre of Oldsmar, Florida now handles the huge bibliographic index of books available in Canada. It is called *Books in Print Plus Canadian Edition* and is also available on CD-ROM. The CTA distributes the Bowker microfiche to Canadian stores.

It is essential that your book be included on this database and is yet one more reason for having an ISBN. Here's why: you live in Toronto and have just published a book titled, *The Politics of Canada's East-West Split.* You send a copy to the book review editor for the *Globe & Mail* newspaper. The editor calls for an interview and before you know it, a huge story appears in the Saturday edition, distributed across the country. A Vancouver businessman reads the article with great interest and wants your book. He calls up his local bookstore and asks if they stock it. The businessman provides the book title, your name and "thinks it's Canadian." The bookstore manager checks the computer to find it is not listed in the store inventory and makes the correct assumption that it is a very new book. The manager's next step is to check his Canadian version of *Books in Print* on CD-ROM. A second or two later, he finds the listing and tells the customer that this book was just released and can be ordered immediately. If you had not submitted the Advance Book Information sheet available from R.R. Bowker, this story would have a very different ending. The manager would simply have said, "I'm sorry, sir, we have no listing for that book. If you'd like to leave a number, we'll do what we can to find it for you." Whether the store staff can afford the time to track down unlisted books is another matter.

If you use a distributor, check to make sure your book information is submitted to the Bowker database as a normal part of the company's business routine. If you are filling out the form, be sure to include your distributor's name in the space provided on the form. Listing with R.R. Bowker will increase your potential sales by making specific ordering information about your book easily available to bookbuyers across the country.

PROMOTIONAL SHEETS AND BROCHURES

When you are publishing, you need a sales tool for providing information to many people. Promotional sheets or brochures are silent salespeople and help sell your book by either announcing its imminent publication or by informing a specific market about its content and appeal. Preparing a promotional sheet before the book goes to print is simple and inexpensive. This is particularly true if you have done your own production work and have access to a photocopier. An advance mailing of a promotional sheet can generate sales.

The example on page 88 will give you an idea of what I mean by a promotional sheet. A rough cover design can be reproduced until you have finalized your cover. Although most people in the book industry accept the fact that the pre-publication retail price is sometimes not the actual price on publication, you should print "approx." after the price just in case, due to unforeseen costs, you have to change it later. Whether you send out one or two advance mailings will depend on your budget (mailings are expensive) or the length of time it takes to actually get your book back from the printer. Marion and I were invited to give a workshop on self publishing at Vancouver's *Word on the Street* festival before this book was due for release. This was a perfect opportunity for selling books but we had none to sell. Instead, we handed out advance promotional sheets to the audience. This gave them a physical message that our book would help them much more than the workshop. It was also a reminder that our book would be out soon and could be ordered now through their favourite bookstore. The idea of promotional sheets is to stimulate advance orders. After this event, I had calls from Vancouver stores wanting to place our new book on order who hadn't already done so. No doubt this was the result of our promotional efforts at the workshop.

You can utilize your book cover to develop a really effective promotional piece. This will require some planning with your printer. Most printers print more covers than there will be finished books. These are called *cover overruns* and you should always request these. Paperback covers are very effective when sent to prospective buyers and far less expensive than an actual book. Extra dustjackets printed for hardcover books are also necessary, both as a sales tool and for re-covering damaged or hurt copies later. To turn your book cover into a working brochure, have the overruns printed on the blank side with sales and ordering information. These are truly useful promotional pieces. By using your cover overruns, you save an enormous amount of money relative to what it would cost to develop a colour brochure. Another option is to have your printer add a lighter weight of paper stock to the bottom of the stack of paper used to print your cover. Since the press is already set up for your colour book cover, the costs of printing the same image onto lighter paper stock will be minimal. Once this is printed, you can have the other side imprinted with black ink on a smaller press. The lighter weight of paper will be easier to fold to a smaller size than the stiff cover stock and you'll save on mailing costs as well.

Order forms are often a part of the promotional piece and are usually directed at specific markets. How you design the order form will depend on whether you plan to direct mail to households, individual consumer groups or whether you are after the retail or library market. Booksellers tend to be philosophically opposed to publishers soliciting sales from the general public and view this as direct competition. Cookbook publishers often include a consumer re-order form in the back of their books. I know booksellers who will tear these forms out prior to stocking the books on their shelves. This is not so unreasonable; they want their customers to do their repeat purchasing through them. Don't alienate those who may become your prime sources of income and, although direct mailing to households can be profitable in the short run, you need to consider the long term benefits of supporting the retail market. One way of stimulating orders for bookstores is to include a phrase such as "Available from your local book store or direct from..." This will encourage the average buyer to look in the bookstore first. If the store hasn't yet ordered, the request may lead to a store order for you or your distributor. If the store still chooses not to order your book, the customer may order directly from the publisher.

Most distributors insist that a new book be accompanied by a promotional sheet of some kind. The distributor uses the sheet as a selling tool when presenting new books in person and by including it with on-going mailings throughout the year or enclosing it in packaged orders destined for customers within their sales network. Distributors are encouraged into promotional activity by those publishers who support their books with printed sales material.

Key Information

Writing and producing a promotional piece involves the same skills you demonstrated in producing your book. As a printed advertisement for your book, it should look professional and to be convincing in content. The copywriting should be concise, yet enthusiastic. The aim is to inspire the person who is reading it to buy the book. Don't try to oversell the book by making claims that cannot be backed up by the finished product. You have your integrity and credibility to consider. In general the promotional piece should include the following:

1. A brief synopsis of the book with interesting highlights mentioned. Be straightforward and positive while avoiding cliche phrases. Include any excerpts from positive reviews or favourable quotations from notable people.

2. Notes about the author including background that is related to the writing of the book. A book on the medical health care system will benefit from listing the author's medical credentials if that person is a health care professional. In most instances, include the home town of the author on the promotional piece.

3. The book's physical specifications: size, number of pages, format (hard or soft cover) and the number and type of illustrations. Mention the type of binding. Avoid technical printing language such as "Plastic laminated four colour cover". Communicate this by simply stating "glossy colour cover."

4. ISBN

5. Retail price

6. Approximate or actual date (month) of release

7. Your publishing company name and address
   and telephone number
8. Your distributor's name (if you have one already) with a
   toll free order number if available

Leave space on the promotional sheet for the name, address and telephone number of a distributor if you hope to have one at a later date. Otherwise, use this space for the terms of sale such as discounts or minimum order quantities.

DEVELOPING A MAILING LIST

My first experience with direct mail sales was in 1979 when I was selling a drawing workbook to schools across Canada. I knew the school market was the one I wanted to reach, but reaching it started out as a long and slow process of compiling a mailing list. I began in the reference section of the local library and spent hours upon hours writing out school addresses listed in phonebooks and just as many hours thumbing through the pages of the Postal Code books. Whenever friends travelled to a city whose schools I hadn't yet chronicled, I had them retrieve still more addresses for me. I even handwrote each and every address on the envelopes. The saying "Lost time is never found again" took on new meaning the day someone told me that the local school board would give me the one address I really needed. It was the address of an office which promptly sent me a complete list of all the public and private schools in Canada.

I still copy store names and addresses from phonebooks when I am on a sales trip to another city, but for an entirely different reason. There are always new businesses opening that aren't yet entered on the computerized lists available today. In fact, there are thousands of different types of mailing lists available for just about any market you might want to target. Some are available free for the asking. Try contacting specialty clubs and national associations for their membership lists if you want to mail to individuals with specific interests. Other lists will cost money but are usually worth the expense. The Canadian Booksellers Association has a huge mailing list of trade sources that is available at a reduced price after you pay for a membership. There are companies that specialize in selling mailing lists. Their names are listed under "Mailing Lists" in the Yellow Pages of the phone book. These companies use computers to store names and addresses which can be sorted and printed out on request. You can ask them for specific market segments such as bookstores, libraries, college and university bookstores or schools. You should receive a master list plus the peel-off labels at a cost of so many cents per label. This makes a mailing slightly more expensive in terms of cash outlay, but virtually eliminates researching and compiling your own list. This kind of time saving can earn you money by producing results faster. Lists can also be rented. These are supplied as labels intended for one time use only. The labels may be coded by the company that owns them. To duplicate the list can be inviting legal action.

Mailing lists are never complete and you need to add to them as new opportunities and more contacts develop. Keep track of every address you come across that could lead to sales for your first and future books. Try keeping separate lists of different markets or contacts. I have a media list, a bookstore list which is further divided into stores that specialize in specific books such as guide books, self-help books or cookbooks and a list of wine shops and wineries that I keep for a winery book I once published. The winery list was very useful when, as a distributor, we signed an agreement to sell the Blue Moose publication, *BC Wine Country*. Keep a list of all those who ever buy a book from you. This "bookbuyers" list can be worth money to you in the future when you publish your next book. Separate lists help maximize your cost efficiency by allowing you to target select groups when selling by mail.

Computers save time. If you have a computer, buy a mailing program and start entering addresses every spare moment you have. Some invoicing programs allow you to add to your mailing list without starting new accounts for each name. You can buy the tractor feed labels or laser printer labels and use these in lieu of purchasing pre-printed ones from a mailing list company. If you don't have a computer, use a card file to keep names and addresses catalogued and up to date. To shorten the time it takes to do a mailing manually, type your lists onto sheets of peel off business labels. This master list can be photocopied onto blank sheets of the same labels. It means using a photocopier with a single sheet bypass that will accept different types of paper, but these days most copiers have this option. Then copy the original onto plain bond paper and file it for later use. Since the spacing remains constant, it will match the labels when you copy them again.

MAILING SAMPLE COPIES

Sample copies are an essential part of promoting a new book. Consider that at the annual Canadian Booksellers Association trade fair (the CBA), some of the national publishers give away as many as 250 copies to promote a single new title. Their reasoning is that if they can get the book into the hands of the bookstore owners or staff, if the book is read and enjoyed, the bookstore is more likely to promote that particular title or author to their customers. The publisher and author will benefit in the long term.

Many who publish for the first time are afraid to give away free copies. The pressure of paying for the publishing costs is certainly a factor. You don't have the capital base of a national publishing house, so be judicious about the number you give away. Never hesitate to give a book away if you think it will lead to large sales in the future. I once gave a copy of a book to the sister of a customer who regularly places large orders through my distribution company. As it turned out, the sister worked for a time share company. The following Christmas, the time share company placed an order for $20,000 worth of that same book. If a bookseller asks for a copy it means that person is interested, but wants to decide on ordering after the book is read. Generally speaking, if you feel a sample copy might result in a sale—or a review—at some time in the future, don't hesitate. Keep track of these copies and remember that they become tax deductible expenses.

It is not usually feasible to mail a sample copy to every bookstore. I know of one publisher who sent sample copies to many of the largest privately owned bookstores and was successful in getting their attention, and their orders. The book in question was a small gift book with a retail price of $6.95. If you are publishing a more expensive book, consider saving this cost for media copies where you are likely to generate free advertising for a wide audience. Media reviews and interviews will ultimately benefit the bookstores and you with repeat orders.

BOOK REVIEWS

Newspapers, magazines and radio stations are all sources to contact if you want to have your book reviewed. Prepare a list and group the media outlets that reach the largest number of people. Send a sample or review copy to the editors, reviewers or producers of outlets that can provide national coverage. Include a brief covering letter to the person who regularly deals with books or specializes in your book's topic. Enclose a press release for additional information. Include your business card and, in the case of newspapers, a black and white photograph of yourself. This is called a *press kit*. Prepare the same kind of kit, minus a book, for smaller, regional media. Include a book cover instead. If you later receive a request for a book in response to one of your regional mailings, be sure to send it promptly. It's a bit like fishing: if your regional press kit results in a bite, sending a book ought to land the interview. Always follow up your mailing with a phone call to the people to whom you sent information. Books sometimes end up in hands other than the ones for which they were intended. Perhaps the person was on holiday. Your phone call might inspire the reviewer to make a point of locating your package. Be aware that reviewers receive many packages in the mail.

Book reviews are worth money because they attract attention to the book and result in orders. This kind of print promotion has a lasting effect. A review published in the spring edition of a special interest magazine may be discovered by a potential customer while sitting in a doctor's office a year later, long after the initial response has subsided. Newspapers are extremely effective and widely read. Where broadcast media tends to rely on its immediate listening audience, printed publications have an extended time element that can increase the potential advertising impact of a review. A positive review in a widely read publication will have immediate sales results, as will a radio or television interview. But bad reviews will also earn attention and orders by raising the curiosity of buyers. Some people insist on making their own decisions about some controversial topics. A media person who criticizes a book can stimulate a response from readers who want to know the details of your topic first hand. The more reviews you manage to get for your book, the more people will notice it—including the booksellers.

DEVELOPING A PROMOTIONAL STRATEGY

Promoting your book to every potential market seems overwhelming. If you have a local or regional book, start where you are and build your sales and promotional efforts over time. Capitalize on your prime market. If you publish a book about Nova Scotia that arrives back from the printer in late November, don't rush off to promote it in Toronto before you've promoted it in the area where it is most likely to sell. The risk of recovering the costs of a trip to Toronto in a short period of time is too high, not to mention the difficulties in getting books into the stores at such a late date in the Christmas shopping season. Concentrate your focus on the area where you will receive the greatest and fastest financial returns for your efforts. As you penetrate the local market, begin a direct mail strategy to bookstores or special interest groups. You can always make that trip to Toronto during the spring book buying season in February or March.

SEASONS

There are buying and selling seasons in the book industry. Publishers announce upcoming titles and release new books in spring and fall. Promotion takes place well ahead of the publication dates to encourage advance orders. This helps publishers determine the size of their press runs based on the quantities ordered. It also gives them publishing deadlines to meet.

Bookbuyers want to anticipate their customers' needs. Books for spring, summer and fall may be ordered as early as December, January or February. Late winter and early spring can be the best time to introduce your new book on gardening or hiking. Ordering in advance of seasonal demands allows *lead time*. Retailers want publicized new books in their stores early to take advantage of every possible sale. This is particularly true for the Christmas shopping season. Books for sale at Christmas are ordered in June or even earlier. The buyers may specify a delivery date of early September or October and will be influenced by the type of promotional campaign set out by a publisher. These are national buying trends. Retailers can and do purchase new books on a year round basis. If you are publishing a children's Christmas story, consider having it out as early as January or February.

PERSONAL PROMOTION

Almost anything you can do to develop an awareness of your book is considered promotion. Don't go anywhere without at least one copy of your new book and when people ask you what you've been up to lately, start personal promotion by telling them about it. Word of mouth is a powerful form of promotion in book selling and shouldn't be disregarded. As Marion said at the beginning, it is important to be enthusiastic because it's your enthusiasm that will motivate an individual to go out and buy your book.

There are endless opportunities for personally promoting your book. Read the newspapers, listen to event calendars on the radio and be alert to media stories about special events that might provide an opportunity for a table or booth where you can display or promote your book to large groups of people with related interests. Seasonal festivals also provide good opportunities to personally present yourself and your book to the public.

No one can promote or sell your book better than you if you really believe in your product and can promote it well. In the publishing industry, promotion is the primary domain of the author and publisher. The publisher will normally cover the costs of print promotion (mailers and space ads) and make their best efforts to gain media publicity for the book and author. It is the author's responsibility to be available for interviews or signings and this responsibility is generally a clause in the publishing contract. As a self publisher, both author and publisher, the compounded task of arranging print promotion, media interviews and making yourself visible to the public falls on your shoulders alone.

APPROACHING BOOKSELLERS

Approaching booksellers is another form of personal promotion. Your visit will have much more impact than even the most expensive brochure or the most enthusiastic sales representative. When your book arrives, take it down to your local bookstore. You might give the owner or manager a personalized copy as a small token of appreciation for help you've received. Also ask if they would be interested in having you do an in-store signing. You may hear two questions that will be repeated over and over by almost every bookseller you approach about signings: "What kind of promotion are you going to do?" and "How much co-op advertising money is available?" What most booksellers want to hear is that you have arranged for publicity in the form of media interviews that will not only announce the publication of your book, but will also inform the public that you will be in that particular bookstore for a special launch promotion and signing on a given date. The concept of co-op advertising dollars relates to a policy maintained by many commercial publishers. If a store is prepared to run an advertisement announcing a new book or an author's appearance in the store, publishers will contribute an amount of money towards the cost of the ad. Most stores are satisfied with an amount ranging from $30 to $75. This depends on the size and ad rates of the chosen newspaper. You must decide whether to support the bookstore in this. It has become an expected aspect of signings in recent times. Most bookstores put some effort into promoting an upcoming signing: they want to sell your book just as much as you do. Contributing a small amount of money towards this common objective is not too much to ask.

Personally promoting your book to bookstores doesn't mean offering to do a formal signing at every one, but if you are asked, make your best effort to be there. Do go into as many bookstores as possible, even if it means visiting them while you're on a holiday in a different area. Introduce yourself and present your book. There's a good chance the store manager can be encouraged to order if you seem professional and she likes your book. Be polite and to the point. Don't get hostile if the manager decides not to purchase. There may be a good reason why an order can't be placed.

Some store policies dictate that all single title purchases must be made through a known book distributor for reasons of discounts, returnability and reduced paperwork. Many bookstores cater to a specific clientele and it may be that books on your topic don't appeal to their customers. It's interesting to note that many bookstores cater to a specific clientele. Books which sell in quantity at one store may not sell at all in a store just blocks away. Some bookstores maintain a wider selection of literary titles or nonfiction business books or perhaps self-help/motivational books depending on the type of customer base they have developed over the years. So if you have a literary title and approach a bookseller with a self-help or history focus, she may refuse to buy for this reason. Some stores are identified by publishers as being "poetry friendly" to denote those that stock a wider selection of that genre than most. If a bookseller chooses not to order, remain calm and find out why, then go about finding a new approach that will put your book on those shelves.

While the buyers for small, privately owned bookstores seem not to mind an occasional unannounced visit, it is a practice not welcomed by the buyers for larger stores. Always phone ahead and make appointments with them. Some of these buyers prefer that you send a sample book with copies of press releases, a promotional itinerary and purchasing information. This package can then be followed by a phone call. Self publishers who drop in on a busy buyer can experience the grief of on-the-spot rejection. If you are granted an appointment, be on time with your material organized. Give your presentation in a professional manner. Be brief, positive and confident.

SIGNINGS

The whole idea of a signing is to sell books for the bookstore. Often a store owner will place an advertisement in the paper before you arrive, a newspaper reporter will interview you at the signing and the story will appear in the paper after you leave. Even if no one comes to your signing you have gained publicity in the local paper two weeks running. At your signing, talk to those around you. Be charming, witty and do everything you reasonably can to get a book into the hands of a customer and up to the cash register. This is your job while your are at the bookstore.

A first signing can be traumatic. No one comes. Or no one talks to you. A common experience is a two or three hour stint during which you come to feel as if you've either become transparent or stricken with a rare form of infectious disease. It doesn't mean that you or your book is a flop. It's more likely to mean that most people are quite shy and often don't know what to say or do when they see an author in a bookstore. You can make it easier by making eye contact, smiling and trying to engage them in casual conversation, just as if you were a real person. Another reason for a customer's reluctance is the feeling that if he speaks to you, he is automatically obligated to purchase a book. These are just aspects of being human and you shouldn't take such behaviour personally.

Simply sitting at a table waiting to autograph your books is a very passive situation. With a little imagination, you can create more interest if you incorporate an activity or bring a display or something interesting that is likely to engage a passerby. Cookbook authors might bring baked goods or appetizers to offer customers.

Cultural anthropologist, Dr. Pamela Peck is the author of the *Cannibal's Cookbook*. Far from what you might think, this is a series of cultural essays that demonstrate how ancient rituals are still in evidence on a subliminal level in today's society. Dr. Peck brought many interesting items to her signing including a fork modelled after ones used in cannibalistic societies. The fact that she was able to raise the curiosity of passersby enabled her to engage people in conversation leading to sales of her book. Marion and I promote our signings as free information sessions or seminars: we welcome anyone with questions about writing or publishing. We did this very successfully with the first edition, and I suspect it will work just as well with the second. The point is to bring an extra dimension to the signing.

When the signing session is over, no matter how many copies were sold, be sure to autograph the remaining books on your table. Take a piece of light cardboard and print the title of your book across the top of it. Underneath the title, write "Sorry I missed you" and then scrawl your name across the bottom. Make your letters fairly large and exaggerate your signature so the sign can be seen from a distance. Prop this up on the table with your books and hope the bookstore owner has the space to leave the display up for a day or two. You'll catch sales from people who didn't make it to the signing and from those who might have been too shy to approach you at the time. This is particularly successful close to Christmas when people are looking for very special gifts. The fact that the customer didn't witness your signature seems to have little meaning. In my experiences in coordinating signings for many authors, I've found that as many and usually more books sell in the days following than sell during the signing.

TRADE FAIRS

Trade fairs are excellent opportunities for promoting new books to people within the book industry. Trade fairs are not open to the general public. They are a forum where publishers, sales reps and distributors present their books to the bookbuyers (most of whom are booksellers when they are back in their bookstores).

Regional trade fairs usually take place twice a year in late winter and mid-summer. The dates are scheduled to allow the presentation of new books for the spring and summer selling season or far in advance for the fall and Christmas season. The Canadian Booksellers Association sponsors the national trade fair (the CBA) which is traditionally held in June of each year. The date is set to allow enough lead time for ordering and shipping prior to Christmas sales. Many of the books that are promoted here have not yet been published but have fall release dates scheduled.

To exhibit at a book industry trade fair, you must pay a fee that can run from about $250 upwards to rent a table or booth for a two or three day event. Because retail store buyers are your main audience, your time will be well spent and much more cost-efficient than if you tried to visit each bookstore, city by city, at the outset. You may wish to share a table or a booth with another self publisher or small publishing house to save money.

There are many ways to gain attention at a trade fair. Cookbook promotions have been very successful and cookbook authors go to a great deal of effort to draw people to their booths, offering free samples of cookies, cakes, drinks or appetizers. Colourful balloons, flowers, posters and printed T-shirts or pull-overs are other sales gimmicks that have been used successfully to attract attention. To promote his title, *The Hunter's Tip Book* at a national trade fair, author Bob Marchand supplied about a hundred wooden deer calls to give away to our customers. He also supplied camouflage cloth, an elk call, bear 'perfume', a painted deer skull and two dozen brightly feathered arrow shafts. My job was to take additional copies of his book and combine all of it in an eye catching display in one area of the Sandhill booth. We went even further with a couple of toy bows and arrows with velcro tips to have customers shooting at a fabric target. It was fun; people got involved and we wrote many orders for the *Hunter's Tip Book* at the trade fair.

Some publishers have turned to the use of video monitors and computers to present on-the-spot visual advertising for specific titles. If you don't have a video machine, you'll be in with the majority of publishers who simply promote their books by speaking

117

to individuals on a one-to-one basis. Be prepared to give some books away to interested potential buyers.

Don't expect to sell books for cash at a booksellers' trade fair. It is frowned upon. At the same time, be aware that with changes in buying habits, few booksellers are likely to place orders with single title publishers at this kind of industry trade fair. Think of a book trade fair as an introduction to buyers; view the experience as a way of making your book and yourself known to them. Also keep in mind that these trade fairs open other doors, from making contact with distributors and independent sales reps working the fair to book reviewers interested in new publications. Have business cards ready and bring press releases with you. Give them out with sample copies to any reviewer who shows an interest. Reviews mean sales and that's what you want.

Specialty and consumer trade fairs can be lucrative if you've published a book on a topic such as fishing or home improvement. There are hundreds of specialized trade fairs going on all across the country. Sports shows, home shows, gift shows and even festivals with exhibition halls are all areas to investigate. If you've published a book on canoeing, you'll catch a prime market of individuals with that interest at a Sports and Outdoor Recreation Show. It's usually acceptable and profitable to sell books at consumer trade fairs.

PUBLICITY

Publicity such as newspaper articles or radio and television interviews should be done after the books have been placed in bookstores. The publicity is supposed to motivate the general public to search out the book at their local book outlets. Some sales can be lost if a customer looks for your book and doesn't find it the first time. Some customers may ask for it, others may not. The buyer may forget the name of the book and only vaguely recall the gist of it within a week. So technically speaking, distribution should be the first order of the day after publishing.

The double bind in this industry is that many bookstores won't place an order for a self published book from an unknown source until a customer, or sometimes several customers, specifically ask for the book by title. The bookseller may check *Books in Print,* and order it if your book is listed. This means you sometimes have to gain some preliminary publicity to stimulate and demonstrate the public demand for your book. After distribution is underway and you're satisfied that the largest, if not all stores have stock, pull out the stops and really get to work arranging more publicity. If you do it this way, the chances are you'll re-capture those sales and more.

ARRANGING MEDIA PUBLICITY

There is no magic in getting yourself an interview in the newspaper or on the radio or television. It simply amounts to dedicated work on your part. Media people are constantly on the look out for new material that will appeal to their audiences. If you or the topic of your book fit their particular or general interests, they'll want to interview you.

Ironically, one person who has worked tirelessly at getting media is the author of a book called *The Joy of Not Working.* Ernie Zelinski calls himself the "King of Leisure", yet he has managed to garner more free national and regional publicity than many authors promoted by the publicity departments of Canadian publishing giants. His secrets as I see them are time, research, perseverance, preparation and follow up. Innovation is also foremost in his mind. His first book, now out of print, was called *The Art of Seeing Double or Better in Business*, a book aimed at stimulating creative and innovative thinking. To get the attention of radio producers and newspaper editors, Zelinski cut his books horizontally in half and sent just the half copies in his press kits. This ploy worked and resulted in book reviews, radio interviews and television spots. Without cutting the books in half, Zelinski managed to parlay his publicity for *The Joy of Not Working* into sales that have well exceeded the 50,000 copy mark. The authors of a cookbook also used innovation to get national radio exposure on CBC's *Vicki Gabereau Show*. Using the idea of late night talk show host David Letterman's top ten list, the authors had an artist make up large sign boards citing the ten reasons why Vicki Gabereau should have them on her show. It worked for them.

You, too, can arrange your own interviews with television or radio personalities. Start in your home town with local radio stations, newspapers or television stations. Being in the spotlight in your home town is sometimes less intimidating and can serve as an excellent practice ground. Go to the library and ask for the reference book that lists Canadian media and contact names. Do your research. Take the time to analyze where and to whom to send your media packages. By utilizing your press kit and following up with phonecalls, you'll be well received by many people in the media industry who will be happy to interview you.

You can hire a publicist to arrange interviews for you. Publicists are people who offer their services to secure a set number of media interviews for authors. Publicist's fees range from $25 an interview to $150 - $750 per day depending on the services and media interviews provided. The publicist might arrange five interviews in a combination of newspaper, radio and television spots. Publicists will sometimes accompany you to the studio, encourage you, make suggestions on what the interviewer likes, and tell you how well you did after you have finished. Some publicists just arrange interviews, leaving you to find your way to the addresses provided. If you opt to hire a publicist, be sure to discuss exactly what services will be delivered and what additional expenses will be charged to you. Expenses include long distance telephone calls, letter writing, courier services and/or car rental. You might be charged an extra hourly rate if the publicist picks you up from the airport and accompanies you to your interviews. Some publicists include those services in their daily charge. You can also negotiate a package of three days or one day once a week for several weeks. Publicists run their own private businesses and adjust their services and fees to individual clients. If everything is discussed in advance, there should be no surprises when you receive a bill for services.

It is difficult for a publisher who doesn't deal with the media every day to keep a current list of media personalities and to know the kinds of material they are looking for. A publicist may know that a certain radio station is planning a series of programs using local gardening writers. The small publisher who has just published a gardening book may not realize this radio opportunity until the program airs on the radio—far too late to participate in it. A publicist who has dealt with the same program director or interviewer many times will have the advantage of an established business relationship. It is also sometimes difficult to sell yourself, the author, as an interesting personality. It seems uncomfortably like bragging. It is easier to arrange publicity through a publicist, but it is possible to do so without one.

120

PRESS RELEASES

Press releases are essential when approaching the media. Press releases are not the same as promotional sheets which are focused on a sales market. A press release is written so that it can be reprinted with minimal editing by a newspaper. Have the words "For Immediate Release" in large type at the top of the page followed by the date. Begin your press release with a simple interesting heading. For the book, *Voyagers of the Chilcotin*, about a couple who moved from California to the wilds of British Columbia, I began a press release with the heading, "Bella Coola Bound." This was reprinted as the heading in several newspapers. Write your press release in a positive, up-beat style with the objective of catching the reader's interest and making that person want to read the entire book. If you've written a book on literacy, for example, begin your press release with some facts on the status of literacy in Canada to give a general context, then follow with the reasons why your book is essential to the cause. If you can whet the appetite of an editor or program director, your interview will be assured. Don't make the press release any longer than a single page or you may lose the interest of a busy program director. At the end of the body copy, include the names of local retail outlets carrying your book or specify where the book can be purchased in general terms: "available at local bookstores" and quote the retail price. As a separate item at the bottom of the page, list again the title, author, publisher and size of the book along with the date of release and the price, just as you did on your promotional sheet. This gives the person receiving the press release all the pertinent details at a quick glance. Be sure to include your name, your company name and a telephone number where you can be reached for additional information or an interview confirmation. It is sometimes advantageous to include the name of your distributor.

WHERE TO SEND YOUR PRESS RELEASES

Choose media outlets that have wide coverage areas so that you can reach as many people as possible with a single interview, but at the same time, don't underestimate the importance of small town newspapers or stations. They tend to have very steady and loyal audiences whose response can make a great difference to your sales. Send sample copies with your press kits to the larger companies as well as to any journalist who seems particularly aligned with your topic. Approach all your local media outlets in person or by telephone. Design a self-addressed response card that can be included in mailings to small coverage areas or places that seem not quite as likely to be interested. If they want to do a feature, the response card is a convenient means of contacting you for a sample and further information.

SOME TIPS ON MEDIA INTERVIEWS

The media people I know admit that some authors are easier to interview than others. They can usually tell within a few minutes whether an interview will go well or not. Very shy, quiet individuals pose a particular challenge to radio and television interviewers. Authors who always answer questions with monosyllables will not earn points or a return invitation from a radio host who is left filling dead air with his own voice. Many interviewers will ask one leading or general question in hopes that the author will go into an explanation or anecdote that will be interesting to the listeners. If you have never been interviewed it may help to prepare a small card on which you have written key words that you think will be of interest. I have heard interviewers say that their guests sometimes have difficulty focusing on answers to specific questions. Listen carefully to the questions and try to answer them. Seldom are you asked embarrassing questions. The interviewer usually wants you to do well. Don't say negative things about your own book and try not to agree with an interviewer who says negative things about it. Be sure to mention the full title of your book, particularly in radio interviews. Don't say "My book on trees," say "My book, *A Guide to Backyard Trees*." You want listeners to be able to ask for your book by title at the bookstores. Mentioning the name of your publishing company or your distributor will also help.

Newspaper people are under constant pressure to meet press deadlines. I try not to contact a daily paper before 1 pm. In the morning everyone tends to be scrambling to meet their deadlines; then they're off to lunch. It's best to call ahead and make an appointment; at the same time find out the name of the person who does the interviewing in your field. If you self publish a cookbook, it makes sense that you'll want to see the food editor. Otherwise, ask whom you should see. If possible, have some good quality black and white photographs taken of yourself and bring them with you to the interview. An article with a picture has a better chance of being run than an article without a picture. Always dress for the possibility of being photographed at the interview since many newspapers will take their own photos anyway. Some newspapers allow you to make separate arrangements with the photographer to purchase copies of pictures for your promotional use after the paper has run the article.

SPACE ADS

Investigate the cost of advertising in your local newspaper. Ask a bookstore owner if a co-op arrangement is possible when your book is published. This can encourage them to place an ad in the paper and your book will receive additional publicity.

There are many magazines, book trade journals and tabloids that offer advertising space to publishers. The *Canadian Bookseller*, *Quill & Quire* and *BC Bookworld* are just three of many. Write and ask for their rates. How effective an ad will be depends on your book, your ad and the readership targeted by the magazine or journal. One publisher said that she had tried space ads in a variety of publications with little success. The best response to an ad for her book came from one placed in Toronto's *Globe & Mail* book section. Other publishers have had success with space ads in specialty magazines. If you have a fishing book, a hunting book or a guide book, try advertising in magazines that appeal to outdoor sports enthusiasts. You can code your return address to monitor mail order results. You should keep records to analyse whether the cost of advertising is recovered in the value of orders received. It is disappointing to pay $200 for an ad and only receive $20 worth of orders. As a distributor, I see a different response to books advertised in specialty magazines. These are the orders we receive from bookstores with customers who have seen the magazine ads and want to buy through the bookstore. The most recent books published by John Garden of Footprint Publishing are very large, very expensive railway books. John advertises his books in railway hobby magazines. While John certainly receives many orders from individuals and hobby stores, the bookstores and my distribution company have also benefited from his advertising dollars in the number of people who are aware of these books and buy them. These are the sales that are harder to measure than the ones received directly by the publisher.

Most self publishers don't have large advertising budgets. They rely on book reviews and media interviews to provide what is essentially free advertising. The cost of a 20 minute radio interview would be prohibitive if you were billed by the station's advertising department. Do research advertising rates in a variety of publications, but don't stop seeking out as much free advertising for your book as you can.

BENEFITS OF MEDIA PUBLICITY

Large orders can be a direct benefit of publicity. Chainstore bookbuyers require a printed itinerary of past, present and future publicity for new books because, generally, books that are well publicized, sell. The scope of publicity can influence the size of an order place by a bookbuyer for a large store or chainstore. If, for example, you have commitments from three different prime time CBC radio shows to air coast-to-coast with reviews appearing in national newspapers, it's possible to receive an initial order for as many as 500 books or more from one chain bookbuyer. Without major publicity, these kinds of orders are unlikely. In their eyes, yours is an unproven book from an unknown publisher. Still, the buyers are aware that publicity creates demand and they'll want the books in the stores to satisfy their customer requests and increase sales. Other opportunities can result from media publicity. One interview can lead to others. The producer of the Oprah Winfrey Show read an interview with Marion in the *Baltimore Sun* and called her. You may receive invitations to speak at group meetings or to teach a course on your topic. Publicity can lead to publishing offers from larger companies.

SUSTAINING YOUR MARKET

There are weak links in the publishing, promotion, sales and distribution chain that must be constantly watched for breakdown. Beware the "flash-in-the-pan" syndrome when books are heavily publicized as they first appear, but receive no more promotional attention once they are out in the bookstores. Heavy advance and

124

launch promotion will gain initial orders, but your efforts must continue over time to keep the books selling and to prevent them from coming back in boxes from the stores.

Repeat publicity is absolutely essential to sustain sales over time. It doesn't mean going back to the same interviewers who featured your book in the beginning. It can mean going back to the same television or radio station and talking to another interviewer with a different program. You might present a new idea based on one aspect of your book that wasn't previously covered and which ties in with the theme of a second radio show. In addition to the major national media outlets, there are all of the local or regional media outlets to contact. There are so many possibilities for additional publicity that you can easily plan a year long promotional schedule. Magazines are good sources of on-going print promotion. Try to get reviews in as many magazines as possible. Propose story ideas based on your book, but approach each idea from a different angle. If you write an article for a magazine, try to negotiate for either an inset or a mention of your book as a part of your writing agreement. Use every opportunity you can to continue promoting your book. At the same time, be sure to stay in touch with the bookstores or your distributor and keep them informed of additional publicity. This on-going contact will help to stimulate re-orders. If you convince the booksellers that you are serious and committed to helping your book sell, you'll gain credibility and respect. It takes time, money and hard work but books rarely sell without on-going publicity.

THE INTERNET AS A FORM OF PUBLICITY

The Internet is a fascinating, potentially useful and definitely exciting communication system that has added new marketing dimensions for authors, book publishers and booksellers. Many bookstores have been quick to take advantage of this cyberspace real estate in establishing website addresses. One is able to browse through book lists, publishers' catalogues, author profiles and reviews, to choose and to order books, without ever leaving the comfort of a home computer. There are now huge on-line bookstores such as the American Amazon mail-order service and our Canadian *Chapters.ca* Internet site that are both seeking to test the sales and profit potential of the book industry on the Internet.

The success of the Internet as an effective sales tool has yet to be proven to many publishers. There are many questions regarding this form of mail order shopping. Will it replace today's traditional bookstore shopping where books can be physically handled and purchased quickly? Will it lead to the demise of printed books and replace them with words and pictures on computer disk? Many, including myself, doubt either scenario will come to pass in this generation. Large and small presses are investigating the Internet as a sales tool, nonetheless. Murphy Shewchuk, owner of Sonotek Publishing spent a considerable amount of time and money to have his titles available to the public on the Internet. He is discouraged by the sales results he has received. He believes that the Internet is "an interesting way to reach the masses,—but whether the masses *want* to be reached is the question." It is a passive form of shopping that relies on the individual to voluntarily enter the system via computer and then to act on the information received.

The Internet as an advertising and promotional vehicle for books is more promising. I think of it as another form of space advertising, much like ads placed in magazines or newspapers. There are now lots of companies that design "web pages" or the electronic files formatted especially for use in the Internet system. These files are placed in specified locations within the Internet and accessed by an Internet address. Like an ad, the information you see on your computer screen can be printed out so it has physical form. Some may choose to order books via the Internet. Others will check with their local bookstore for more immediate availability. It is an option in the world of promoting and selling your books.

A word of caution: remember that anything you send onto the worldwide web is open to copyright violation given the tremendous difficulty in tracking or enforcing your legal copyright. If you place a chapter of your book in the Internet system in hopes of attracting a potential book buyer, you have given it away. This raises serious implications for all authors and publishers. If you'd like to research the Internet more thoroughly, there are many, many books written about it. Ask at your local bookstore—or try the Internet.

PART SEVEN:

Sales and Distribution

Nancy Wise

Jillhilly Publishing
123 Anywhere Street
Writersville, Canada EY2 4EP
Ph: 250-763-1406
Fax 250-763-4051

INVOICE

INVOICE NO: 123

DATE: January 16, 1997

Bill to: **Ship To:**

CUSTOMER WHO PAYS THE BILL   **STORE THAT ORDERED BOOKS**
Street Address   **Street Address**
City, Province   **City , Province**

SALESPERSON	P.O. NUMBER	DATE SHIPPED	SHIPPED VIA	DISCOUNT	TERMS
Jill H.	5634	January 13/97	Canada Post	40%	Net 30 days

QUANTITY	DESCRIPTION	RETAIL	AMOUNT
10	HOW TO SELF PUBLISH AND MAKE MONEY	$16.95	169.50
	Less 40%		- 67.80

SUBTOTAL	101.70
SHIPPING	2.58
GST	7.30
TOTAL DUE	**$111.58**

Make all checks payable to: Jillhilly Publishing
If you have any questions concerning this invoice, call: Jill Hill 250-763-1406

BN #12345678910

THANK YOU FOR YOUR BUSINESS!

How to write an invoice in the book industry

Selling Books   **10**

DIAL 911

I once received a phone call that demonstrates the prudence of researching sales and book distribution before you go to print. It was a call of quiet desperation: "I'm sitting in my livingroom surrounded by 19,000 copies of my new book. I need *help*!" This self publisher had spent three years lovingly creating the text and illustrations of an 18 page children's book with apparently little time spent thinking about distribution. It wasn't until she was confronted with the physical mass of 19,000 books that the next step of having to sell them became an overwhelming reality.

THE DAYS OF WINE AND ROSES

Huge first printings are daunting to the best of us. Be realistic in your expectations of how many copies will sell in one year. Reprinting is a much better option than succumbing to the temptation of increasing your print run to lower your per book cost. Before you print your book, talk to a distributor or someone in the sales end of the industry. If you plan to handle your own sales, you must understand that the days of selling large quantities of books from the trunk of your car are over. Sure there are exceptions, but the exceptions are very rare now. Generally speaking, the selling of self published books to bookstores by author/publishers has become a much more difficult task in the nineties. There are a number of reasons for this, but first you need to know the three standard retail purchasing requirements or "standard trade terms" that are still basic to the industry.

STANDARD TRADE TERMS

These are the basic rules that have traditionally been followed in the selling of Canadian trade books.

1. Booksellers in the retail sector require a standard 40% discount off the retail price. This is the minimum discount they expect. While some booksellers accept lower discounts, they are the exception rather than the rule. Large volume orders based on single title quantities (all of the same book) are usually placed with an expectation of a slightly higher discount ranging from 41% to 45%, or 50% if purchased non-returnable.

2. Booksellers expect a minimum of 30-60 days to pay for their orders. Very large bookstores will demand 60 to 90 day terms. National companies such as Chapters, Inc. (the corporate name for the company that owns all of the stores operating under the names of Smithbooks, Coles, Book Company, Chapters superstores and more) demand these extended terms because they represent a huge buying power. A chainbuyer can place a single order for all of their branches at once—a kind of volume purchasing that independently owned bookstores cannot match. The longer terms also relate to the length of time it takes for an order to arrive at a bookstore. An invoice can arrive at a store long before the order does.

3. The books must be returnable. The book industry is a high risk business. Booksellers will minimize their risk by insisting that if a new book doesn't sell, it can be returned to the supplier for a credit against the future purchase of other titles from that supplier. By normal standards, books that don't sell must be returned within one year from the date of the invoice, in new condition so the books can be re-sold to someone else. Whether the books are re-saleable

is a current issue under scrutiny by buyers and suppliers. The booksellers reason that if a book has been in the store for 9 months, if it has been handled by customers at all, it cannot possibly go back to the publisher in perfectly mint condition. The bookseller has done his or her part in making it available to the public. Some large publishers are recognizing this and choosing to accept these returns which may later be sold at a reduced price as hurts or remainders. Many single title publishers sell these at low prices at special events such as public speaking events, consumer shows or craft fairs.

The business implications of accepting returns form a part of the underlying rationale in the reluctance of booksellers to purchase directly from individuals as opposed to large suppliers. Take the instance where a bookseller buys 10 books from a first time publisher on net 30 day terms. After 30 days, the bookseller pays, even though the books haven't sold through. After 6 months, the books still haven't sold and the individual who sold them has disappeared into parts unknown. The bookseller may be saddled with books that will never sell. Buyers that are once stung are twice shy about paying for books in advance of sales.

CHANGES IN BUYING TRENDS

If there are two key words that describe the changes in buying trends within the bookstore market over the past decade, they are the words *computerization* and *consolidation*. Since the late 1980's, computerization has been the major trend in bookstores of all sizes and kinds. Software programs are now in place that can tell a bookseller what they have in stock without having to send a staff member to look on the shelves. *BookManager* is one widely used program that has become an essential tool for Canadian bookstores. Booksellers were once faced with physically counting the number of copies in stock of a particular book. They had to watch sections and know which titles were selling and which ones were not. They had to remember the details of titles, prices and buying sources for their books. Sometimes they lost money because they forgot they had had books in the store for longer than a year, the maximum time allowed by publishers who might otherwise have accepted the unsold books back for credit. Today, computerization coupled with management software like *BookManager* and *WordStock* allows a bookstore owner to know exactly which books are selling and which books are not with a few strokes of a keyboard. With this kind of inventory, sales and ordering software in place, booksellers have become much more efficient. They are more conscious of their profit margins and costs because they can see exactly where they stand financially at any given moment.

From a bookseller's point of view, consolidation simply means buying as many titles as possible from as few suppliers as possible. There is a greater awareness of the time and real costs associated with handling books: staff members must be paid to unpack boxes, receive shipments on computer, stock the books on shelves, complete and file the paperwork, and later to reconcile invoices and credits to statements and of course, issue cheques to each supplier. Buying many books from fewer sources makes the time spent more cost efficient.

Prior to automation, booksellers had their staff physically count specific sections, shelf by shelf, book by book. In a large store, the business book section, for example, might only be counted once every six weeks due to time and staff constraints. Larger orders were placed to ensure they would have enough stock sufficient for the six week time period between stock counts. Computerized inventory management, point of sale scanning, increased speed of ordering and faster delivery of shipments from larger suppliers are responsible for the change in the inventory levels a store must now carry. Because a bookseller can see exactly what has sold on a daily, weekly, monthly and yearly basis through the use of a computer, some of the guess work has been taken out of the ordering process. The ability to gauge when and how many books to order to ensure that the new inventory arrives just before the old inventory sells out, is called "just in time" ordering.

PROBLEMS FACING SELF PUBLISHERS

The changes in book buying trends have made it increasingly difficult for self publishers to profitably sell their own books to bookstores. Booksellers are more aware of the time and costs associated with buying one title from one individual. They are more inclined to order two or three copies to try, than in the mid-eighties when quantities of ten or more were common. There is a greater insistence on consignment terms from single title publishers. This means that they will stock your book, but only pay you if the books

132

sell. Some booksellers are pessimistic even about consignment sales. The argument is that if the bookseller agrees to place three copies of your book on the shelf in January, and in June you arrive to ask for payment, only one copy may have sold. The bookseller views his time spent finding the original consignment invoice, calculating what is due and producing a small cheque as a large cost in relation to a small profit on one book. You have not made any money either given your time and cost in getting to the bookstore.

As discouraging as that may sound, many single title or self publishers do make money selling directly to retail accounts. Booksellers are often the first to admit that they rely on you to produce unique books and books of local interest that might not otherwise be of interest to larger publishers. Few booksellers will turn away a self publisher who has just produced a professional looking, well priced book on some aspect of their local area, or a book that caters to a demand already present within their customer base. The nineties also have seen a great reduction in the amount of government funding available to large, commercial publishers. Book lists are being cut as a result and fewer titles by new authors are being produced by these full time publishers. Self publishers and single title publishers contribute greatly to the pool of Canadian books available to booksellers. Many of you will be successful; some of you will not be as successful. In either case, you must get on with the business of knowing how to sell your book.

HANDLING SALES: SMALL PRESS RUNS

Although you may encounter resistance from some bookbuyers, it certainly is not impossible to handle all of the sales of your book. If you have produced a short run book of just 1000 copies, you usually cannot afford distribution options for your first printing. This means approaching and selling your books to buyers, delivering or shipping orders, invoicing, collecting money and doing regular call backs to stores to replenish their stock. Most of all, it means an excellent opportunity for learning through personal experience. By going through these steps, you'll gain a better understanding of all the various aspects involved in physically placing your book in the marketplace.

Although it depends on the subject of your book and many other variables, a thousand copies is a relatively small quantity to sell if you live in a densely populated area. Organize yourself by making a list of stores you plan to contact, grouping them according to areas in order to make the most of your time and your gas expenses. A numbered triplicate invoice book from an office supply store is necessary and sufficient to get you started. Have a rubber stamp made up with your company name and imprint the invoices with it. Take a supply of business cards so stores will know how to get in touch with you. Take a pocket calculator. Load the car with your books and set off to get them onto bookstore shelves.

CONSIGNMENT SALES

For most self publishers selling their own books, offering consignment terms is the only way some booksellers will agree to accept these books for sale. Most stores will not take the risk of paying for books that are unproven. At one time, the standard discount for consignment terms was 30%, recognizing that you were essentially financing the books in advance of sales. Today, booksellers are now demanding 40% for consignment titles. While many people do not like this form of selling, consignment is one way of demonstrating the saleability of your book. If it sells well and consistently, you will be in a better position to discuss standard purchase terms. Stay on top of your consignment accounts and be sure to check back regularly in person or by telephone, both to re-stock and to maintain good relations with your customers.

GUARANTEED SALES

If you have published a book that is in great demand because it capitalizes on a much needed idea , you are in a better position to adhere to the industry's standard trade terms. This means invoicing for sales based on standard terms with payment due in 30, 60 or 90 days. Be warned that if your book doesn't continue to sell well, the bookstore owner may decide to treat your net 30 day invoice as a consignment invoice. You will be expected to accept returns if a bookstore does not sell all of the books ordered after a period of time. If you have just published one book, you will have no option but to give a cash refund. This becomes a point of honour if you have promised returnability. The book industry is based on trust and ethics. Be sure to keep an amount of money set aside, just in case.

HOW TO WRITE AN INVOICE

Invoices for books are based on the percentage discount to the penny. Although it seems easier to round off a wholesale price of $5.98 per copy to an even $6.00, this practice will instantly label you an amateur in the book business. It will also make it awkward for stores with computers that calculate discounts to the penny. The correct way to write an invoice is shown in our example on page 128. Multiply the number of books by the retail price of the book. Multiply this number by 40% and then subtract the discount amount from the first number. This is the subtotal. If there is a shipping charge, add it to the book subtotal. If you are a registered GST vendor, you must add the 7% tax to the combined total of books plus the shipping amount. You must also show your GST vendor number or the newer federal Business Number (BN) on your invoice. Add all three amounts to reach the total amount payable.

When you receive a store order, you'll often discover a purchase order number on it. This is a reference number used by the purchaser to keep track of authorized orders. It is also used in accounting departments to verify the accuracy of orders received. Always write the customer's purchase order on your invoice. Sometimes you'll be asked for invoice copies in triplicate. While you should use numbered, triplicate invoice forms with one copy for the customer, one for your accounts receivable file and a back up copy, don't send all of your copies to a customer. Photocopying the original twice and stapling the three of them together will do the job. Libraries and schools appreciate the extra effort.

If you have invoices custom printed, be sure they are sequentially numbered for accounting and tracking purposes. A packing slip can be designed as the fourth copy if printed in carbonless sets. Packing slips are identical to invoices except that no calculations appear on them, other than the retail price. Packing slips are important if you receive an order that has one address where the books are to be shipped and a separate address for billing. Send the packing list with the books after photocopying it. Attach the copy of the packing slip to the invoice and mail it separately. Always be sure to read your orders carefully and to follow billing and shipping instructions as well as order cancellation dates.

If you plan to stay in the business of selling books yourself or if you contract with suppliers, consider a computer accounting program that will generate invoices, track your inventory and the money that is owed to you (your accounts receivable). It will save hours of bookkeeping and guessing as to where your books have been sent. This is particularly important with consignment sales which involve receiving payment for just part of the original order. If you use invoices created from a template in a software program on your computer, be sure to print in multiple copies so you always have a hard copy duplicate for your files.

GOODS AND SERVICES TAX

Registering as a GST vendor is only necessary by law if your expected annual business revenue will exceed $30,000. Many small publishers fall under the threshold and opt not to register. Earning less than $30,000 per annum does not mean that you can't register and there are some advantages if you do. You can register as Jill Hill doing business as (dba) Jillhilly Publishing. As you sell your books, you must invoice your customers for GST as a registered vendor, noting your Business Number on your invoice. Once registered, you become a tax collector, but you can also claim refunds of GST on expenses associated with running your publishing company. Instead of remitting all of the GST you collect to the government, you can deduct from it the GST paid on your business expenses within the filing period chosen. Most importantly, the GST you pay on your printing bill becomes a credit in your favour. You should register with the GST office before you begin your book project (although there is some leeway on your start up date) and master the accounting aspects of being a GST vendor.

At the time of writing, there is a movement to harmonize provincial taxes with the federal GST. Lobbying efforts are underway to fight the addition of further taxation to the book industry. Check with your local taxation office for the current status of this issue.

SHIPPING CHARGES

The government once subsidized the shipping of books as cultural commodities. Book Rate was a special rate for publishers available from Canada Post. This rate was eliminated some years ago. Today, single copy orders that are under 500 grams will go as First Class mail or via Parcel Post if heavier than 500 grams.

Bookstores are usually billed for shipping by small presses unless you have agreed otherwise. Large publishers, wholesalers and distributors sometimes absorb shipping costs as an incentive to purchase. They are often forced to absorb them since the chain bookstores will not normally accept shipping charges. Distributors seldom pay shipping charges on books received from publishers because they are faced with the costs of moving the books out into the marketplace.

Including your invoice inside a packaged order is the easiest and most cost efficient way of handling your billing. To do this, you have to calculate the shipping charges before you seal the box and take it to the Post Office. Using a metric weigh scale and the charts supplied by the Post Office is the simplest option. If you don't have a weigh scale, you can calculate shipping charges in advance. Take a few books to the Post Office and have them weighed. You may discover that one book weighs just under 500 grams and two books weigh just under 1 kilogram. Have the postal clerk tell you the best rate for each. To be more accurate, allow for the weight of a box, packing material or padded envelope. You can then use your calculator to determine shipping charges without a weigh scale or you can program the rates into your computer. If you find that you are shipping a large volume of books on a continuous basis, then investigate trucking and delivery services. CanPar is a door-to-door business delivery service that is widely used by the book industry.

PACKING ORDERS

If a customer receives your books in less than perfect condition, they will be returned to you—at your expense. Before packing, examine the books carefully for printing imperfections or damage. Keep in mind that a box of books passes through many hands while being transported to its final destination. Boxes get thrown, dropped, squashed and compressed in piles of other boxes. As a general rule, pack each order as if it were going to be used like a football.

Protect your books with packing material to cushion them inside the shipping carton. You can purchase unprinted roll ends of newsprint from your local newspaper or large bags of styrofoam chips from an industrial supply house. Avoid using any printed newspaper since the ink will come off on your books. Use cardboard, cut to size, to reinforce boxes and to protect book corners.

Buy packing tape at a wholesale house. You may have to buy a large carton of it, but it is much less expensive this way than by the roll. For small orders, use padded envelopes also available in bulk quantities through shipping supply wholesalers or stationery stores. Alternatively, cut two pieces of cardboard slightly larger than the book size and sandwich the books between them. Then wrap in heavy duty brown paper and tape well. Use your computer to generate shipping labels. Alternately, you can have mailing labels custom printed or you can rubber stamp peel off labels available through industrial suppliers.

MAKING SALES PROJECTIONS

Selling the first copies of a book you have created is truly exhilarating. By the time you've sold the first few hundred, the feeling is euphoric. It is a wonderful experience, but be careful. Don't make sales projections based on the number of copies first placed in stores. Because books are returnable, many people in the industry feel that a sale is not a sale until John Q. Public buys the book and takes it home. I love people who eat and read at the same time because I know of no bookstore owner who will exchange a book with peanut butter and jelly on it.

The ideal scenario to reinforce your dreams of success is to distribute approximately half of your press run in the area where you live. As you promote and publicize the book, 500 like-minded people rush to the bookstores to purchase copies. Soon, the booksellers are phoning you to re-order. When the re-orders come to you, you know the first batch of books has gone out of the store and are bona fide sales. At this point, you can begin thinking about your next printing while evaluating numerous variables. Think about your publicity (will it continue?), your area of distribution (will the book sell in other regions?) and your finances (can I afford another print run? should I increase the quantity?). Although some conjecture is inevitable, try to use the hard evidence and market indicators you have observed while selling your first print run without being unduly influenced by dreams of independent wealth. Remember that printers can supply reprints quickly these days; don't go to reprint until your inventory is very low or even sold out.

138

HANDLING SALES: LARGE PRESS RUNS

If you publish a large number of books you must move your book into the bookstores quickly. You want to convert your investment in books back into cash as fast as possible. Achieving widespread distribution as a self publisher is difficult, particularly if you are new to the industry. It takes time to develop sales contacts and time to become known as an ordering source. If you are dividing your efforts between doing media interviews and selling, you'll have a difficult time developing sales relationships and establishing a good reputation for filling orders quickly.

There are several types of sales and distribution methods commonly used by publishers with large press runs. Sales reps, distributors and wholesalers will help move your books into the stores. Each will have an established sales network. They will have on-going sales relationships with the chain bookstores. Sales reps, distributors and wholesalers sell books as a full time occupation and will continue their sales efforts for the length of your agreement. This gives you time to get out and promote your book or to write and publish another.

Booksellers will often advise you who to contact and provide phone numbers. The *Canadian Publisher's Directory* is published by *Quill & Quire* magazine and is available in libraries. It contains a list of publishers as well as the names and addresses of the distributors, wholesalers, and sales representatives based in Canada. The *Book Trade in Canada*, published annually by Ampersand Communications, is another excellent source book.

THE SALES REPRESENTATIVE

A sales representative (or "book rep") can be an employee of a book sales company or can work independently as a self-employed individual. The rep may cover bookstores in a specific geographic area and may represent one or many publishing houses. This person carries catalogues and sample books supplied by the publisher and presents these to the bookbuyers. When an order is placed with the rep by a bookseller, the sales rep looks after sending the written order to the publisher. The bookseller receives the order direct from the publisher with an invoice.

There are variations in the way sales reps work in Canada, but generally, they are not involved in physically filling the order, nor are they involved in billing. The commissions paid to book reps can vary. Many work on a 10% percent commission taken from the net invoiced amount, or the value of the book order after the store discount. Some are paid a base salary, with their commissions added once they have achieved a certain sales level and an annual bonus incentive added when predetermined sales quotas are reached. A publishing company may hire many sales reps to sell their books in an attempt to get as much market penetration as possible. However, they are usually careful to protect each rep's territory in order to allow the rep to establish relationships with the buyers and to maintain sales motivation. The rep will usually receive a commission on all sales originating in a defined territory whether the rep actually writes the order or not. A bookseller may decide to order as a result of a visit, yet delay placing the order until later. The buyer may place re-orders for books initially promoted or sold by the book rep. The rep is creating an awareness of the publisher's books just by keeping in contact with the accounts. These efforts are worth money to the publisher.

Having a sales rep for a single title can be a good decision, providing you can find a sales company that will take your title or someone who is skilled in sales and dedicated to your book. The rep must also have a reasonable expectation that your book will generate enough commission to be profitable. There are a number of independent sales reps who take on a wide line of books from medium, small and independent publishers and who travel specific regions on a regular basis. Book reps, like distributors, are often oriented to specific markets, selling to either bookstores or schools, but seldom to both with the same energy. There are also library reps who deal specifically with library purchasers.

Dealing with a sales rep or a sales rep company means that you will handle all of the shipping and invoicing. There may be some resistance from booksellers who will prefer distributors and/or wholesalers for the cost efficiencies of combining orders. If you opt for the repping system, you will need time and some workable facilities for processing the orders either in your home or a small warehouse space. You'll have to develop an efficient billing and accounting system and pay the rep according to the terms agreed upon. Where there is an exclusive agreement, you will be required to pay the sales rep a percentage of all the sales within the agreed upon territory. This includes sales that you make within that territory. If you have published a cookbook, you may wish to contract with a rep for sales to bookstores only and cover specialty accounts such as cooking stores yourself. Some agreements with sales rep companies require that the publisher pay a percentage of all sales made to wholesalers or libraries in addition to the bookstore market. As with all business contracts, read the fine print and discuss the details until you are satisfied with the agreement.

DISTRIBUTORS

Finding a distributor in Canada who will take on a self published book is not always easy. There are few that will deal with single title publishers. Booksellers will tell you which distributors they feel are active and reliable and which ones provide them with good service. You can phone bookstores in various regions to find out which distributors they recommend. It is quite usual for them to recommend a distributor that is located near to them since they are more likely to know the distributor and the staff personally. This is also an indication that the distributor is giving them good service.

Good distribution requires a co-operative effort between the publisher and the distributor. The average industry discount required by a distribution company is 60%, of which the distribution company will keep 20% gross profit after standard bookstore discounts. The 60% discount may seem like highway robbery at first. You might feel that you have just spent a year of your life working on your book with all of your life savings used to publish it. Now you discover that strangers may potentially make more money on it than you will. It isn't until you have attempted to do your own distribution that you become aware of just how much is involved in the work of a distributor. Distributors solicit orders in numerous ways. Distributors will make personal sales calls to promote the books they carry and may employ sales reps in much the same way that publishers do. They attend trade fairs and often special events. Orders are also solicited through telemarketing and extensive mailings. Travel expenses, reps' commissions, trade fair fees, telephone charges, and postage are just a few of the sales related costs borne by the distributor. The company keeps stock on hand to consolidate and ship orders. Warehouse space is costly, as is the labour required to fill the orders. Since distributors also invoice their retail clients, they are required to maintain a detailed bookkeeping system. In addition to sending statements and collecting invoiced amounts, a book distributor must also keep track of sales and make payments to those they represent. Consider a large distributor with several thousand accounts and representing some 200 publishers, each of which may have an average of thirty to fifty titles, if not more. It's a big job.

Very large distributors often concentrate all of their time and efforts on large commercial publishers for economic reasons. It was once explained to me that for the amount of time the company spends talking to one person with one book, they could as easily spend the same amount of time promoting their services to one commercial publisher who has a hundred books. Another big advantage that large publishers have from a distributor's viewpoint is the fact that these publishers are constantly producing new titles each season to add to the distributor's list, much like a brood mare in the thoroughbred breeding business. While no one in the publishing business forgets that many large publishers started with one title, self publishers initially tend to produce an average of only one book every one to two years. Rather than searching out new titles to increase their lists, it is easier and more profitable for large companies to maintain a stable of active commercial publishers. This doesn't mean that there are not distributors out there who will welcome your book, but it can be the reason behind a negative response if you approach a very large company. Search out those distributors that specialize in single title or small press books. Remember that distributors with fewer titles often have more time and energy to devote to promoting and selling individual books.

It is important to acknowledge and recognize the long term benefits of having a distributor. Booksellers feel more confident about stocking a book available through a distributor. Knowing the supplier as an established ordering source in the industry will reduce their perceived risk on an unproven title. The distributor will encourage re-ordering on a continuous basis over time. As the distributor's reps work through the list of available titles with a bookseller, attention will be given to your book. When asked, a salesperson can advise the customer of your book's general sales performance and offer recommendations on order quantities.

Eventually, your book and the distributor become identified with one another in the eyes of the bookseller. This link is essential to fostering identification and making re-ordering books easier for booksellers. One of the worst things you can do is to leap frog from distributor to distributor, confusing bookbuyers. If they place an order for your book through your first distributor, this distributor may or may not direct buyers to the new source for ordering and is under no obligation to do so. If you change your distributor, you must be sure to notify as many stores as possible, giving the new ordering information. If you change distributors more than twice, many stores will not bother to search out your latest supplier.

Having a distributor means working together to sell your books. Keep your distributor informed of promotional events you are planning so that the company can be sure the stores have stock. Also keep bookstores informed by means of regular mailings and phone calls about your promotional activities. While you want to stay in contact with your distributor, don't make unnecessary demands on the distributor's time or patience. I know a self publisher who was taken on by a very large distribution company. She plagued them with phone calls every week asking how many books had sold and wanting to know every account where the books had been placed. Eventually, the company decided that her phone calls were more trouble than they had bargained for. They returned all of her books with a polite note observing that she obviously felt they were not doing their job and that she should seek the services of another distributor.

Let the distributor handle the job of selling books and try to help in any way you can. You will sell more books if you co-operate than if you complain. Consider that the distributor wants to make money on your book, too. Don't treat your distributor like a competitor. If your agreement states that the distributor handles orders from bookstores, it isn't fair to continue actively selling to them. You might fill an order to a store ordering for the first time and enclose a note to the bookbuyer informing him that additional copies are available from your distributor. However, the bookstore will appreciate it more for reasons of consolidation and accounting purposes if you forward the order to your distributor. Likewise, if you are in a store that has sold out of your book, talk to the buyer and take the re-order on the spot. Give the order to your distributor.

This method allows an excellent opportunity for you to promote your book to the bookstore while demonstrating your professionalism. Since a distributor can't be in all places at once, don't antagonize the distribution staff by accusing them of not doing their job. It is possible that the last copy was purchased moments before you walked into the store. It is also possible that the store owes money to the distributor and has been placed on a credit hold pending payment of their account. Communicate with your book supplier. If you support your distributor and work with the company, they are likely to work that much harder at selling your book.

PARALLEL LINES OF DISTRIBUTION

In certain situations, it is not uncommon to have two separate distributors, but only if each distributor handles a completely different market segment. It is not normal to have two distribution firms selling your book to bookstores. This can lead to confusion on the part of the booksellers and poor relations with both book distribution companies. It is a courtesy to discuss other distribution avenues with your bookstore distributor prior to signing a sales agreement. I once signed an agreement with a self publisher in good faith. Two days later, she called to say she had also signed with another distributor. I immediately voided our agreement on the basis of principle. I was angry knowing that this person had negotiated an agreement with us without mentioning a second agreement signed with another company. This is unprofessional conduct in an industry based on ethics and good faith.

The entire retail market is made up of many different segments. There are distributors that specialize in specific markets other than bookstores. Someone who has published a fishing book will want this book in both bookstores and stores that cater to anglers. There are distributors that specialize in fishing products and sell primarily to fishing stores. There are also distributors that specialize in health food stores, gift shops, building supply stores and more. You might find an educational distributor that sells to teachers and teacher-librarians. This does not mean that a trade book distributor will not also sell to these markets. It simply means that some companies will focus their efforts to a greater degree on certain market segments.

WHOLESALERS

Distributors are different from wholesalers, who tend to service grocery stores, gas stations, drug stores and to a lesser degree bookstores. Wholesalers usually carry mass market paperbacks and magazines, with trade books making up only a small percentage of the titles carried. Wholesalers will buy books on a net 90 day returnable basis. Their discounts are usually lower than a distribution discount. This is because wholesalers offer an in-store shelf stocking or rack jobbing service for which they charge the customer by giving less of a discount. Where a wholesaler will take a title in at a 50% discount, they will in turn give their customers only a 20-35% discount. Although it seems as if they will sell your book for less, they are still making as much or more than a distribution company.

There are many types of wholesalers, from ones that service the bookstore market to ones that service libraries and schools. Where distributors sign agreements with specific publishers to distribute their list of books, wholesalers carry almost anything that their retail customers request. At one time, it was believed that bookstores should be the primary sales outlets for trade books. There was a great deal of controversy several years ago when grocery stores began to sell trade books. Today, the retail market boundaries have become more diffuse as large stores of all kinds now regularly stock trade titles. Many of these stores are supplied by one wholesaler who can offer a wide variety of titles and provide racking services not available from individual suppliers. It is another form of consolidating orders deemed to be more profitable than the administration required to manage many suppliers.

There are many regional wholesalers to whom you can submit your book for purchase. This can be a good way to get into non-traditional or specialty accounts and is a method to be used in conjunction with a trade book distribution company. If you opt for an agreement with a wholesaler, be very careful to specify that you will accept "whole book" returns only. It is a practise with some wholesalers to tear off the book covers and return these to the publisher for credit. This occurs primarily with mass market paperbacks, but I have known it to happen to trade paperbacks. Also discuss turn over with the wholesaler to find out how long they will leave your books on the shelves. Wholesalers are known for quick returns. You want to make sure that your books don't get cleared off the shelves at the end of the month along with dated magazines.

TAKE MY BOOK, PLEASE

I see very little difference between submitting your book to a retail bookbuyer and submitting it to a sales company, whether it be a sales rep, a distributor or a wholesaler. You must still convince someone else that your book is wonderful, unique and will sell in quantity if put on the shelf. Some research and thought will be required to determine the best markets to pursue with your book. You will want to put together a *sales kit* which is essentially your press kit plus copies of newspaper or magazine reviews that you may have received. It is very important to also develop and include some kind of marketing plan to show that you have some ideas on what you can do to promote your book in the future. Add a covering letter explaining why your book is wonderful and include a detailed list of the kinds of people who will want to buy a book on the topic you have chosen. You must not forget to include the specifics of retail price, publication date and the size of your print run (some companies will not accept books with very small print runs).

Next, call various sales companies and suppliers that have been recommended by your local bookstore. You should be aware that no matter how brilliant and saleable you believe your book to be, it is a buyer's market at this level of the book industry. (Distributors, wholesalers and sales reps will make it clear that it is they who decide whether they will take your book or not.) Talk to the person in charge of acquiring new titles. Ask questions. Ask first whether the company deals with single title publishers. If so, does the company specialize in particular types of books such as fiction, non-fiction or cookbooks? Does your book fit into their categories? Which geographic areas are served by the company? Which sales markets? Ask what the company's terms are and what discounts are required. If you've been successful in getting this far with positive responses, you can ask for an explanation of their payment system.

If you've spoken to a distributor who seems interested, send a copy of your book along with your sales kit. Make it look as professional as possible and include a cover letter with your address and phone number. Since trade book distributors sell to the retail market, they will be looking at the book from the same perspective as a bookstore buyer. Be sure to call back and follow up on your submission to the company. (Many books have crossed my desk that I might have been convinced to carry had the publisher called. It's a sad fact that these books get set aside as "maybes"—no one calls and the business of selling other books takes precedence.) If your follow up call leads to a verbal agreement for distribution, you can expect to receive some form of distribution contract that will outline how the company operates in terms of stocking your title, how payment will be made and how returns will be handled. Different companies will have slightly different terms, conditions and stipulations that can be discussed before you reach a final agreement for services.

PATIENCE AND PERSEVERANCE

Regardless of whether you have a sales rep, a distributor or a wholesaler to sell for you, it takes time to build a market for a new book. If you are not in the enviable position of having an instant runaway bestseller, have patience and perseverance. It can take three to six months just to get the books into a significant number of stores and up to a year or more to develop a widespread awareness and demand for a particular title. It is said that a work of fiction only has one year to make it or break it in establishing itself as a steady seller. Regional books and non-fiction seem to have a much longer life span. It can take as long as two years to develop the desirable situation where your book becomes part of a "Basic Stock" store list or a book that is regularly re-ordered on a continuing basis. This is the ideal when bookstores come to recognize the sales value of a title and routinely order it to satisfy a consistent public demand.

The Last Word

It *is* possible to make money. Occasionally a publisher produces a book that flies to incredible heights: coast to coast sales, curriculum adoptions, foreign rights sales and a movie contract. This is the rare occurrence that beckons all publishers. Good management, thorough research and assiduous pursuit of the market can produce a profit on your book, but your book to be saleable must be well-written, of good design and well-produced. With the advent of desktop publishing, a small print run is now more economical and therefore more possible than in the past. There are many self published books serving local interests. This enriches our culture.

Canadians have an international reputation for interesting books of good quality. All publishers, large and small, need to feel a responsibility to the established reputation of Canadian books. Every publisher, from McClelland & Stewart to a self published author publishing for a local market, needs to feel a dedication to these standards of excellence. We hope that this book has made you aware that those standards exist and that you will contribute to and benefit from them.

If this information makes you decide not to self publish you may have saved much time, effort and money. You may also have gained an understanding of the publishing business which will allow you to write for a market that is of interest to an established publisher. It may help you prepare for a career in the book industry. If you decide that you have the time, energy and money, as well as the necessary compulsion to publish, go ahead and self publish. We promise you that it will not be dull.

Be prepared to be obsessed by your project. All your ideas, plans and activities will centre on books: your book, other publishers' books, foreign books, back list books and forthcoming books. You will talk to friends and see them as potential customers. You will go out to dinner and try to sell your server a book. You will breathe printer's ink and speak in characters. Life becomes more exciting, precarious, seductive. If you still want to self publish, welcome to the world of possibilities. And good luck.

Addresses

Assn of Book Publishers of BC
100 West Pender, Suite 107,
Vancouver, BC V6B 1R8
Ph: (604) 684-0228
Fx: (604) 684-5788
E-mail: admin@books.bc.ca

Assn of Canadian Publishers
2 Glouchester St., Suite 301,
Toronto, ON M4Y 1L5
Ph: (416) 413-4929
Fx: (416) 413-4920

Assn of Manitoba Book Publishers
(also *Prairie Books Now* office)
100 Arthur St., Suite 404
Winnipeg, MB R3B 1H3
Ph: (204) 947-3335
Fx: (204) 942-1555

Atlantic Publishers Marketing Assn
1515 South Park Street, Ste 304
Halifax, NS B3J 2L2
Ph: (902) 420-0711
Fx: (902) 423-4302

Book Publishers' Assn of Alberta
10523 100th Ave.
Edmonton, AB T5J 0A8
Ph: (403) 424-5060

Canadian Authors Assn
PO Box 419
Campbellford, ON K0L 1L0
Ph: (705) 653-0323
Fx: (705) 653-0593

Canadian Booksellers Assn
789 Don Mills Road
Toronto, ON M3C 1T5
Ph: (416) 467-7883
Fx: (416) 467-7886

Canadian Centre for Studies in Publishing
Simon Fraser University
at Harbour Centre
515 West Hastings
Vancouver, BC V6B 5K3
Ph: (604) 291-5077
Fx: (604) 291-5098

Canadian Intellectual Property Office Industry Canada
50 Victoria St.
Place du Portage, Phase I
Hull, PQ K1A 0C9
Ph: (819) 997-1936
Fx: (819) 953-7620

Canadian ISBN Agency
National Library of Canada
395 Wellington St.,
Ottawa ON K1A 0N4
Ph: (819) 994-6872
Fx: (819) 997-7517
E-mail isbn@nlc-bnc.ca

CIP Program
Acquisitions and
Bibliographic Services Branch
National Library of Canada
395 Wellington St.
Ottawa, ON K1A0N4
Ph: (819) 994-6881
Fx: (819) 953-0291
E-mail cip@nlc-bnc.ca

Editors' Association of Canada
35 Spadina Rd.
Toronto, ON M5R 2S9
Ph: (416) 975-1379
Fx: (416) 975-1839

Independent Publishers Assn of Canada (IPAC)

c/o Script Publishing Inc.
839 5th Ave., S.W.
Calgary, AB T2P 3C8
Ph: (403) 290-0800
Fx: (403) 241-8575

Book Publishers of Ontario

720 Bathurst St., Ste 301
Toronto, ON M5S 2R4
Ph: (416) 536-7584
Fx: (416) 536-7692

Prairie Publishers' Group

5203 Barron Dr., NW
Calgary, AB T2L 1T7
Ph: (403) 276-3162

Quill and Quire

70 The Esplanade, Suite 210
Toronto, ON M5E 1R2
Ph: (416) 360-0044 *Local 346*
Fx: (416) 955-0794
Subscriptions:
35 Riviera Dr., Unit 17
Markham, ON L3R 8N4
Ph: (905) 946-0406

R.R. Bowker
Data Collection Centre

Attn: Canadian Project
Tri-County Business Park
12712 DuPont Circle
Tampa, Florida 33626 USA
Ph: (813) 855-4635
Fx: (813) 855-2309

Writers' Union of Canada

24 Ryerson Ave.
Toronto, ON M5T 2P3
Ph: (416) 703-8982 (Mon-Thurs)
Fx: (416) 703-0826
email twuc@thewire.com

Quick List for ISBN and CIP

For **ISBN:**
National Library of Canada
Ph: (819) 994-6872
Fx: (819) 997-7517

The following is a list of **CIP** offices by region:

for Alberta, BC and the Territories:
c/o University of BC
Ph: (604) 822-6838
Fx: (604) 822-4789

for Manitoba and Saskatchewan:
c/o University of Manitoba
Ph: (204) 474-9476
Fx: (204) 261-1600

for Ontario, minus the Ottawa area:
c/o University of Toronto
Ph: (416) 978-1803
Fx: (416) 978-7457

for the Ottawa area and English publishers in Quebec:
c/o Nat'l Library of Canada
Ph: (819) 994-6881
Fx: (819) 997-7517

for French publishers in Quebec:
Bibliotheque Nationale du Quebec
Ph: (514) 873-1100, ext. 375
Fx: (514) 873-4310

for the Atlantic Provinces:
c/o Dalhousie University
Ph: (902) 494-6687
Fx: (902) 494-2319

150

Index

The following list represents a few of the well known and much used book printing companies in Canada and is provided as a starting point to help you obtain printers quotes. This list in no way precludes the capabilities of other printing houses not mentioned here. Please see the *Book Trade in Canada* published by *Quill & Quire* for more complete listings and information.

Friesens Corporation - Book Division
1 Printers Way
Altona, Manitoba R0G 0B0
Ph: 204-324-6401 Fax: 204-324-1333
Website: www.friesens.com

Hignell Printing Ltd.
488 Burnell Street
Winnipeg, Manitoba R3G 2B4
Ph: 204-784-1030 Fax: 204-774-4053
Website: www.hignell.mb.ca

Marc Veilleux Imprimeur Inc.
1340, rue Gay-Lussac, Section #4
Boucherville, Quebec J4B 7G4
Ph: 450-449-5818 Fax: 450-449-2140

Transcontinental Printing Inc. - Book Division
Toronto Sales Office
505 Consumers Road Ste 401
Toronto, ON M2J 4V8
Ph: 416-492-2711 Fax: 416-492-2533
Website: www.transcontinental.ca
In BC:
1552 W. 66th Avenue
Vancouver, BC V6P 2R9
Ph: 604-263-4700 Fax: 604-263-4710

Webcom Limited
3480 Pharmacy Ave
Scarborough, Ontario M1W 2S7
Ph: 416-496-1000 Fax: 416-496-1537
Website: www.webcomlink.com

For additional copies of *How to Self Publish and Make Money,*
please contact your local bookstore. To arrange author interviews,
special events, lectures or for classroom sets, please contact:

Sandhill Book Marketing Ltd.
#99-1270 Ellis Street
Cannery Row Building
Kelowna, British Columbia V1Y 1Z4
Ph: 250-763-1406 Fax: 250-763-4051